MW00808131

INSIGHTFUL LEADERSHIP

SURFING THE WAVES TO ORGANIZATIONAL EXCELLENCE

JIM TOMPKINS

and

MICHAEL HUGHES

BRIGHTRAY
PUBLISHING

All rights reserved. Published in the United States of America by BrightRay Publishing.

ISBN: 978-1-956464-19-1

www.brightray.com

CONTENTS

PRAISE FOR INSIGHTFUL LEADERSHIP AND JIM TOMPKINS

"Jim Tompkins is a thought leader who has often been able to see the future. My conversations with Jim have always been about what is next, and next. I have experienced this with Jim on topics of supply chains, robotics, technology, eCommerce, Unichannel, and more. Now, Jim has unleashed his power of seeing the future on the topic of leadership. His book on Insightful Leadership is both profound and practical, making it a user's guide to turning chaos into competitive advantage. Thanks Jim, a book I will read several times."

SHEKAR NATARAJAN, EXECUTIVE VICE PRESIDENT, CSCO/CEO (AIRTERRA), AMERICAN EAGLE OUTFITTERS INC., SAN FRANCISCO, CA

"Few can articulate as well as Jim Tompkins how disruptive forces can either sink an organization or propel it forward. With *Insightful Leadership*, Jim has crafted another must read for leaders of any industry."

MITCHELL E. DANIELS JR., PRESIDENT OF PURDUE UNIVERSITY AND FORMER GOVERNOR OF INDIANA, WEST LAFAYETTE, IN

"*Insightful Leadership* combines the best of Thomas Kuhn's *The Structure of Scientific Revolutions* with Geoffrey Moore's *Zone to Win* in the context of 40 years of global business experience to help technology entrepreneurs understand the nature and role of leadership in the 21st century. These insights equip leaders to not only survive the pounding surf of relentless Disruption, but to harness that kinetic energy in ways that propel their enterprises to new heights. *Insightful Leadership* is another example of how Jim Tompkins combines serious engineering rigor with decades of inherited wisdom to address one of the greatest challenges for any organization: leadership. I see *Insightful Leadership* as required reading for all who aspire to lead well at any level of any organization."

G. EDWARD POWELL JR., PH.D., CHAIRMAN,
IPX, NASHVILLE, TN

"Jim has an outstanding ability to analyze and articulate what is going on around us. My interactions with him always leave me inspired to excel and extend my boundaries. We are in a supply chain environment that breaks most of the norms that we have conditioned ourselves to accept. Jim's latest leadership offering equips us to find a pathway through the leadership challenges that we need to confront. Well done Jim – again!"

MICHAEL C. BROWN, MANAGING DIRECTOR,
LOGDESIGN, MELBOURNE, AUSTRALIA

"Retailers truly know that Disruption is the new normal in today's world. Jim's leadership examples and insights, especially concerning Distributed Logistics and Digital Supply Networks, are important reading for any executive or entrepreneur. Among leaders, Jim Tompkins truly is supply chain illuminati who has, once again, provided practical advice on how to handle these challenging times."

MOHAN RAM AKELLA, SENIOR VICE PRESIDENT, WALMART US OMNI-CHANNEL SUPPLY CHAIN, SUNNYVALE, CA

"I've known Jim for nearly 20 years and have followed his thought leadership since my formative days as a supply chain professional. His insight on business Disruption and how to manage through change has always been ahead of the curve. *Insightful Leadership* encapsulates best practices for dealing with a worldwide supply chain that faces eternal Disruption. No longer can leaders just manage through the latest issue – they must build resilience in their supply chains by "seeing around the corners," applying insights, anticipating the next Disruption, and proactively implementing change. Jim details how surfing the waves of an ever-changing environment versus reactively being pushed around by the tides is the way forward to ensure a successful evolution to a contemporary and resilient enterprise."

JAMIE BRAGG, CHIEF SUPPLY CHAIN OFFICER & EXECUTIVE VICE PRESIDENT, TAILORED BRANDS, HOUSTON, TX

"Jim Tompkins and I have been good friends for many years. From the first time I heard him speak at a conference, I was fascinated by his insightfulness. Now almost 40 years later, he has written a book on Insightful Leadership: an amazing read that provides a roadmap on how to turn Disruptions into victories and how to take problems and turn them into strategies. Thanks Jim. Of my many books of yours on my shelf, I believe this is the one I will reread the most."

RIC SCHNEIDER, CHIEF PROCUREMENT
OFFICER AT ABBOTT, CHICAGO, IL

"I have known Jim Tompkins for more than 25 years. When his book *No Boundaries: Break Through to Supply Chain Excellence* was released in 2003, it immediately piqued my interest. This book was truly transformative at the time because Jim described supply chains as an ecosystem without borders rather than a chain of links. Well, Jim has done it yet again! In his most recent book, *Insightful Leadership: Surfing the Waves to Organizational Excellence*, he explains why today's outdated leadership and supply chain paradigms are no longer effective. But Jim doesn't stop there; he also talks about how to be successful in leadership and supply chain post-2020. I recommend this book to all corporate leaders and supply chain professionals."

GREG BRADY, CEO, ONE NETWORK
ENTERPRISES, DALLAS, TX

"From healthcare to manufacturing to supply chain, Jim Tompkins captures that drowning sensation business leaders and entrepreneurs have felt for the last few years. *Insightful Leadership* provides a prescription to handle not only the current changes, but a way to surf this world of continual Disruption into a successful future. Jim has given leaders a necessary lifeline for these turbulent times."

GREG SMITH, EXECUTIVE VICE PRESIDENT,
GLOBAL OPERATIONS AND SUPPLY CHAIN,
MEDTRONIC, MINNEAPOLIS, MN

"Jim Tompkins and I have a lot in common. We both are deep thinkers and have a passion for excellence. When Jim and I talk I often gain new insights or new ways to view challenges. In Jim's new book *Insightful Leadership*, I gain a different view of what has happened to business since the year 2020. Amazing how studying Disruptions can provide you with a preview of what is coming next. A major contribution to the body of knowledge on leadership."

ARTHUR L. VALDEZ JR., EXECUTIVE VICE
PRESIDENT, CHIEF SUPPLY CHAIN &
LOGISTICS OFFICER, TARGET
CORPORATION, GREATER MINNEAPOLIS-ST.
PAUL AREA, MN

"Jim's approach to leadership transcends generations, truly linking fundamentals to today's digital world. Professionals of all stages of their career will benefit from his experience and insights."

CRAIG WEISS, SENIOR VICE PRESIDENT
SUPPLY CHAIN, CONAGRA BRANDS,
OMAHA, NE

"Jim Tompkins' ideas on leadership in a world of chaos are backed by deep analytical thinking and real-life examples gleaned from decades of leadership experience in entrepreneurship and supply chain. I have deep admiration for Jim – he has been a trusted advisor for years – and his new book is full of riveting stories of how we got where we are – and how Insightful Leadership is the way forward in every sector."

VIK SRINIVASAN, CHIEF ADMINISTRATIVE
OFFICER, MEIJER, GRAND RAPIDS, MI

"Jim's newest book gave me insight into being insightful. *Insightful Leadership* will help leaders and entrepreneurs surf the waves of continuing Disruptions. The outcomes are likely to be much better than the impossible task of taming Disruptions. A must read."

YOSSI SHEFFI, MIT PROFESSOR OF
ENGINEERING AND DIRECTOR, MIT CENTER
FOR TRANSPORTATION & LOGISTICS,
CAMBRIDGE, MA

"Jim brings the credibility of a seasoned operator, the insight of a respected mentor, and the curiosity of a continuous learner to every encounter. His latest book, *Insightful Leadership*, again reveals his unique ability to take emerging trends, pressure test them against our existing practices, and imagine radically different future scenarios."

COLIN YANKEE, EXECUTIVE VICE
PRESIDENT, CHIEF SUPPLY CHAIN OFFICER
AT TRACTOR SUPPLY COMPANY,
BRENTWOOD, TN

"I've known Jim Tompkins for 30 years, followed behind him as President of IISE, so I got to work with Jim closely. He's been a trusted colleague and advisor and, in my view, one of the best in class thought leaders in Integrated Systems Engineering—a great mind, great thinker, great leader, and a very successful business developer. I really value how Jim has continued to learn, innovate, and communicate. Jim is great with metaphors, and Surfing the Waves to Organizational Excellence describes how it feels like nowadays in organizations. Jim has a unique ability to simplify things that are complex. His presentations and webinars, particularly those for IISE's membership, are mesmerizing. He's profoundly thoughtful but in a way that resonates with practitioners. This comes out clearly in *Insightful Leadership*."

SCOTT SINK, PH.D., SENIOR ADVISOR, THE POIRIER GROUP, AND GLOBAL OPERATIONAL/PERFORMANCE EXCELLENCE TRAINING LEAD, IISE, SMITH MOUNTAIN LAKE, VA

"Jim Tompkins is a Purdue engineer and entrepreneur who was a leader by the time he graduated with his Ph.D. many years ago. This successful businessman has been a great friend of mine and Purdue University. His book on Insightful Leadership is compelling, and in these challenging times it is an important foundation for startup and grown-up organizations around the world."

MUNG CHIANG, PRESIDENT-ELECT, PURDUE UNIVERSITY, WEST LAFAYETTE, IN

"Jim Tompkins is a pioneer in the field of leadership and a true innovator ahead of his time. His insight to the correlation between the changes we have experienced over the last couple of years as a society and the necessity for change in leadership style are brilliant and matter of fact. The necessity for adaptation, evolution, and mastering the ability to pivot seamlessly are just a few of the takeaways that make this a must read for competitive leaders of all industries around the world."

NICK SANSONE, PRINCIPAL AT SANSONE
GROUP, ST LOUIS, MO

"I've known Jim Tompkins for more than 30 years, worked closely with him when he served on the IISE Board of Trustees, and supported him when he served as IISE President in the early 1990s. As CEO of IISE for the last 17 years, I have very much appreciated Jim's continued strong leadership and support of our Institute and our profession, benefiting our conferences, our publications, our awards and recognition initiatives, and many other areas. I have been amazed at Jim's leadership, entrepreneurship, innovation, enthusiasm, and thought leadership. *Insightful Leadership* has stimulated my thinking, revealing a whole new understanding of how the Disruptions of the last few years impact the future."

DON H. GREENE, P.E., CAE, CHIEF
EXECUTIVE OFFICER, INSTITUTE OF
INDUSTRIAL AND SYSTEMS ENGINEERS,
ATLANTA, GA

"Seeing around corners and navigating the global waves of ongoing and disruptive change with an extraordinary sense of business leadership and acumen is simply what Jim Tompkins has always done, at least ever since I've had the pleasure of knowing him as a mentor and friend. If there is anyone who personifies solution-oriented ingenuity with an eye of creating win-win solutions every time, it's Jim. *Insightful Leadership* ... the perfect title from a leader who always looks to find the best way forward."

VICTOR WATTS, CEO CHAIR, VISTAGE
WORLDWIDE, CARY, NC

"Over the course of the three decades I've worked for, with, and alongside Jim Tompkins, I've grown to appreciate his insightful, inspiring, and authentic leadership more and more. He lifts everyone around him! In this book he shares his experience, business insights, and leadership approaches in a compelling and engaging way. The proposition is simple: Read it, act on it, and prosper!"

PHILIP GREENWOOD, ORIGINATOR,
AUTHOR, AND COURSE LEADER AT DIGITAL
ACUMEN, CEO OF IPSEITA LIMITED,
LONDON, ENGLAND, UK

"Jim Tompkins is a guru who became a friend during years of mentorship that moved me from the corporate world to the entrepreneurial world in the supply chain industry. *Insightful Leadership* again showcases Jim's brilliant ability to pinpoint the tides that businesses are riding on and point out options that can help your enterprise surf forward toward continued success."

"Once again, Jim Tompkins has provided executives and entrepreneurs with practical advice, relatable stories, and concrete examples to deal with the magnitude and speed of today's perpetual Disruptions. Instead of fearing obsolescence, you will come away from Insightful Leadership with the ability to turn chaos into competitive advantage."

"Jim's thought leadership is always ahead of the curve, and my friend has struck again with *Insightful Leadership*. Jim's book is so right – leaders and entrepreneurs must account for the fact that the future is now a departure from the past, not an extension of historical data. Survival in the age of perpetual Disruption will require seeing around corners and surfing the waves – and a lot of hard work to develop your sixth sense: insight."

CRAIG JONES, SENIOR VICE PRESIDENT,
GLOBAL SUPPLY-CHAIN OPERATIONS,
UNDER ARMOUR, BALTIMORE, MD

"I have had the great pleasure of knowing Jim Tompkins for more than 15 years. I have watched him build several successful companies and have always loved his passion for whatever he pursued. *Insightful Leadership* is another great contribution to how businesses achieve profitable growth. The three words that explain Jim's view of leadership are Go! Go! Go! What he means by this is that you should be accountable for doing something good. I love when I get a Go! Go! Go! from Jim."

ALAA MATTAR, MANAGING PARTNER, SC
ADVISORS, DUBAI, UAE

"Jim Tompkins is a visionary who has been out front of the evolution of supply chains, industrial engineering, entrepreneurship, and leadership. Jim has done it again with his book *Insightful Leadership*, laying out the difference between what has worked to what will work. His view on how Disruptions from the last few years have changed how organizations operate is profound and will help many leaders surf the waves to organizational excellence."

ABHIJIT V. DESHMUKH, TOMPKINS CHAIR
OF SYSTEMS, SCHOOL OF INDUSTRIAL
ENGINEERING, PURDUE UNIVERSITY, WEST
LAFAYETTE, IN

"As a follower of the late Clayton Christensen's "Disruptive Innovation Theory," I see Jim Tompkins and his new book *Insightful Leadership* as leading the way to a timely and current perspective on the concept of leading through perpetual Disruption. In our dynamic environment, there is much more than technology driving change. Successful navigation requires a simultaneous balance of anticipating Disruptions, Tipping Points, and Paradigm Shifts and being ready at all times through constant innovation. Jim has led through many business cycles and has continued to disrupt his own thinking to remain a well-respected thought leader and successful business executive."

PAMELA WISEMAN, 30-YEAR GLOBAL
SUPPLY CHAIN AND OPERATIONS
EXECUTIVE, DALLAS, TX

"Jim Tompkins brilliantly captures the current condition of the world based on Disruption. He takes us on an intellectual journey to rediscover life, business, innovation, and success as we ride this wave called 'COVID-19.' There are many powerful insights about leadership that challenge readers to recognize our role in embracing perpetual Disruption as a way to invent a new reality. Simply exceptional."

"I first encountered Jim Tompkins through a business partner. As an academic technologist, I wish I'd found him earlier. He recognizes the human and organizational problems of complexity, uncertainty, and ambiguity in continuous change, but is not daunted by them. Instead, he helps us all to 'peer around corners' and 'surf' waves of Disruption with an inherently agile philosophy. In this book, those habitual practices are the basis of being an Insightful Leader. In the past two years I've seen Jim up close. He is a formidable, truly Insightful Leader, always doing, and doing naturally, what he describes in the book. He anticipates change, acquires knowledge, and influences amazingly diverse teams to happily align and purposely act. The book is a gem."

"Jim Tompkins has been my friend for 30 years, and we have interacted at several levels throughout. His energy, engagement, enthusiasm, and entrepreneurism have always made him stand out from the crowd. Jim's latest book on Insightful Leadership is revolutionizing how we think about leadership. With the level of Disruption that has occurred and will continue to occur, this book is a must read for all leaders desiring to harness the power of these Disruptions for competitive advantage."

LOUIS MARTIN-VEGA, DEAN OF
ENGINEERING, NORTH CAROLINA STATE
UNIVERSITY, RALEIGH, NC

"Jim Tompkins is a trailblazing business leader and holds a Purdue Ph.D. in Industrial Engineering. Jim is a Fellow and former President of the Institute of Industrial and Systems Engineers who received the highest recognition awarded industrial engineers, the Frank and Lillian Gilbreth Award. He has been recognized by Purdue University as an Outstanding Industrial Engineer and as a Distinguished Engineering Alumnus. Jim is a leader, an entrepreneur, a family man and to me, a friend. It is my honor to know Jim and to learn from his latest book. *Insightful Leadership* is a captivating perspective on leadership and management in the post-pandemic world and a book that will become a guide for many."

DR. YOUNG-JUN SON, JAMES J. SOLBERG
HEAD AND PROFESSOR, SCHOOL OF
INDUSTRIAL ENGINEERING, PURDUE
UNIVERSITY, WEST LAFAYETTE, IN

DEDICATION

To all those who were devastated by Disruptions, tripped up trying to find Tipping Points, but powered through to the era of endless Paradigm Shifts.

These are the Insightful Leaders who realize that working from home, the exploding growth of eCommerce, and broken supply chains will not just remain but will be transformed into new paradigms in a world where Disruption is the new normal.

ACKNOWLEDGMENTS

From Jim:

For me and my loving wife, Shari, our three married children and their spouses, and eight grandchildren, like so many others, the last two years have reset our lives. March 2020 disrupted careers, church, school, lifestyle, friendships, and home life. Confusion, uncertainty, frustration, and undesired change threw our lives into chaos. But now, twenty-seven months later as this book is published, I look with gratitude and awe at our family unit. Wow. Here we are, a few scars and bruises, but we made it. Like many others, we stand tall and we look forward. I am proud to be with you, Shari Tompkins; our daughter Tiffany and her family Jamie, Savannah, and Jason Burns; our daughter Jamie and her family Todd, Gavin, and Reagan Heaward; and our son Jimmy and his family Kristin, James, Audrey, Jaden, and Anna Tompkins. I love you.

Jim Tompkins, August 2022, Raleigh, NC

From Michael:

For me, with the best of times still ahead, I too focus on family. Many thanks and much love to my mother, Becky Oglesby Hughes; sister, Theresa Hughes Barnes; brother, Kevin Hughes and his family Melissa, Emery, and Mason Hughes; nephew, Joshua Barnes and his family Christina and Emmaleigh Barnes; and family members too numerous to mention, for their support and understanding. All were deprived of my time while I worked on this book. I truly wish my late father, Floyd Hughes, and great-nephew, LJ Barnes, were here to see this. I also want to thank my former colleagues at IISE, the Institute of Industrial and Systems Engineers, where I first learned about the art and science of supply chain from Jim's Supply Chain column. Of course, I cannot give enough thanks to Jim Tompkins for bringing me on board this wonderful adventure.

Michael Hughes, August 2022, Atlanta, GA

From Jim and Michael:

And to the many partners of Tompkins Ventures and Tompkins Leadership, who daily prove that the power of a network combined with Insightful Leadership is infinite. In a couple of short years, they have grown Tompkins Ventures from one person answering a few phone calls to hundreds of partners solving problems, grasping opportunities, and changing lives around the globe.

Jim and Michael, August 2022, on another Zoom call

PREFACE

Life seemed grim in spring 2020.

COVID-19 patients overloaded hospitals. Death counts rose. People who had owned and worked in "non-essential" businesses, many of them employed at mom-and-pop restaurants and shops started decades ago, were out of work. Bosses were unable to pay business leases. People saw their cars repossessed, their lives upended. Supply chains were fouled as manufacturing and shipping stopped, started, stopped again, and started again.

However, glimmers of hope appeared as we waited for vaccines to tame the rampaging coronavirus.

That restaurant that had been on the corner fifty-two years? The owners transitioned into takeout. Retailers offered more delivery options and curbside pickup. Where allowed, bars mixed drinks to go and offered beer and wine delivery or pickup. Distilleries started making hand sanitizer.

Stories like these started popping up in publications like *The Wall Street Journal*, rays of light breaking through the darkness. For some businesses, these adjustments on the fly helped them live to fight another day. Others were making more money than ever.

The winners, if you can call anybody a winner in a deadly global pandemic, used their insight that this pandemic was not going to end soon. Even afterward, they knew that massive business Disruptions would continue.

Others still did not have a clue about the future. They sat on the park bench, crying, "poor me," or walked around hoping to return to 2019.

That's when it hit me. Disruption is the new normal.

In the past, businesses innovated because they wanted to. Now and forever, businesses innovate because they must. Disruption is perpetual. The solid foundation you rested upon has evaporated into an ocean abyss that will swallow your enterprise.

The thought that Disruption is the new normal, not an occasional glitch, is a disruptive thought in itself.

I could not find anybody saying this no matter how many business and leadership publications I read. They were all waiting to return to "normal" or find a "new normal."

It really bothered me that people did not grasp this trend of VUCA (volatility, uncertainty, complexity, ambiguity), which I started tracking in 2018 and detailed in a YouTube video in 2019. The Black Swan of COVID-19 mated with VUCA, engulfing the old ways of doing business, washing them into the depths.

There is no new normal. The speed and magnitude of Disruption in an era colored by the fallout from COVID-19, not to mention this century's technological innovations and geopolitical and financial crises, will be with us forever.

Business leaders must use insight in the future—Insightful Leadership—not data from the past.

Insightful Leadership will give your enterprise options so you can surf wave after wave after wave across that ocean of Disruption.

Then, it came to me: this is a book. More than that, this is a book based on what I have done my entire professional life—

peering around corners, looking at incoming Disruptions, and aiming to catch the next wave.

My previous company, Tompkins International, started out designing warehouses. As time went on, we added inventory, transportation, network planning, technology, forecasting, implementation, supply chain, fulfillment services, robotics, and so on. At many steps, I was told, "You can't do that."

But I did, going from a backyard startup to one of the world's foremost international supply chain consultancies.

However, as I started outlining the book, writing chapter headings, and sketching notes on notepads, phone calls kept coming. People from my previous business life wanted help with private equity, and somebody always needed help developing the warehouses I used to design. As this grew, my first partner said I could not name our new matchmaking business "answer the phone." So, to write up a partnership agreement, Tompkins Ventures was born.

Looking at my time, I knew I could either continue writing the book or build Tompkins Ventures. But I really, really, really wanted to do both.

The book was important. Not for me—I'd already written or contributed to thirty of them, and I understand everything in this book. No, the book was important for leaders of small, medium, and large companies/organizations; for professionals trying to understand the impact of 2020-2022 on the future; for entrepreneurs making their way through Disruptions; and even for university students trying to understand the future of business.

They were fighting while many other companies were doing no more than moaning and groaning.

That's when I brought in my coauthor, Michael Hughes. He had edited my Supply Chain column for *ISE* magazine for years. He knew the field, and he knew how to write, but he was not overly steeped in strategic planning and other dinosaurs of the past business world. He would not say, "Well,

Jim, the solution is clear: businesses need a detailed five-year plan."

We got down to business. Weekly Zoom calls, torrents of emails, reams of research. I rearranged the book outline at least twice, and overall, the book changed four or five times.

Every time we thought we had something solid, research showed the world had changed again, leading to more rewriting. Some chapters were trashed; others grew into three chapters. When we started, inflation and a Russia-Ukraine war were not on the horizon.

Now, a little more than a year later, it's clear that the process of writing the book validates the thesis behind the book: we are in a world of perpetual Disruption. The future is a departure from the past, not a continuation.

If you think your business plan and operations are set, look around. You are never going to have certainty again. There's another wave coming, so get ready.

1 PERPETUAL DISRUPTION IS THE NEW NORMAL. INSIGHTFUL LEADERSHIP IS THE ANSWER

What is Insightful Leadership? Insightful Leadership has two pillars: seeing around corners and surfing the waves of our turbulent world. COVID-19, digital innovation, and geopolitical and financial crises have accelerated history into a world where Disruption is the new normal. From now on, whatever new normal you finally figure out will soon be swept away by the waves of the future. Instead of optimally designing their businesses, leaders must position their enterprises to catch the waves (Disruptions), navigate those waves when they break (the Tipping Points), use insight into how the waves will advance (Paradigm Shifts), and harness the power of those waves to ride into the future (Innovations).

By 2020, *The Black Swan: The Impact of the Highly Improbable*, by former options trader turned book author Nassim Nicholas Taleb, was on the backburner of many business circles. On the surface, everything seemed fine.

Stock markets skyrocketed.

Businesses boomed.

Successful supply chains spanned the globe.

Despite this, business executives were full of worry. But instead of fearing an unpredictable, one-time disaster (the bubonic plague, World War III, another Great Depression), leaders fretted over seemingly constant volatility, uncertainty, complexity, and ambiguity—a syndrome dubbed VUCA by the U.S. Army War College back in the 1980s.

Changes wrought by the digital era, the disruption cycle, the global economy, innovations from technology, entrepreneurship, robotics, data science, artificial intelligence, geopolitical upheaval, and commerce in general all combined to make 2019 the most uncertain and volatile in world history.

However, as 2020 dawned, top 10 lists of business concerns for the new decade did not include a deadly virus springing out of the Far East to span the globe. But that's what happened as COVID-19 ravaged the Earth, shutting down global economies and creating a new world where more than half (61%) of the United States worked from home.[1] In turn, work-from-home skyrocketed eCommerce sales, sales made possible only by the preceding years of digital innovation. As people feared venturing out, "non-essential" businesses (primary care physicians, restaurants, vacation spots, retailers large and small) cratered.

The cumulative effect of COVID-19, work-from-home, and eCommerce combined with geopolitical and financial crises broke the global supply chains used to deliver goods and services to the world. It reached the point where millions of Americans (and those of other nationalities) cried, "Where can I find some toilet paper?" (The answer came from multiple crowdsourced apps developed to let consumers know where to find toilet paper, milk, sanitizer, and other goods.) The chaos left business leaders, entrepreneurs, and almost everybody else yearning for the halcyon days of the recent past, a past where they could realistically define a sense of normality.

Disruption became the new normal because 2020 was the

year when Taleb's *Black Swan* mated with VUCA. Said union accelerated history and begat massive Disruptions that led to what journalist Malcolm Gladwell called Tipping Points.[2] Those Tipping Points—lockdowns, the eCommerce explosion, and broken supply chains—created what futurist Joel Barker would call Paradigm Shifts, or massive changes in the way we live, work, shop, learn, raise families, and seek entertainment—everything entrepreneurs and business leaders looked to provide. They didn't recede in 2021, when the Ever Given container ship blocked 12% of the world's shipping by getting stuck in the Suez Canal;[3] the Texas deep freeze shut down manufacturing and supply chains all the way to Memphis, Tennessee (including major semiconductor factories); a fire closed a Japanese semiconductor plant that produced 30% of the automotive sector's microcontroller units;[4] a mob stormed past police to interrupt Congress and ransack the U.S. Capitol; and all of this was happening alongside the continuing social upheaval sparked by the 2020 police murder of George Floyd.

Meanwhile, on the COVID-19 front, just as soon as the majority of people were getting vaccinated in a number of countries, the Delta variant reared its ugly head, followed soon after by Lambda and Mu and Omicron and others. Who knows what will come next? Sadly, the virus, too, became a vector not only for sickness, misery, and death, but for perpetual Disruption.

For now and beyond, expect more of this. Recently, China has been saber-rattling about Taiwan, the epicenter of world semiconductor production, and Russia invaded Ukraine again. Inflation has hit levels not seen in generations. Today's leaders must understand that Disruption is the new normal. As we can see from the events of 2020-2022, by the time your enterprise adjusts to whatever you think is now normal, the next new normal will be on the way or already here.

In such a business landscape, what are leaders to do?

The only thing they can do—peer around the corners and surf.

Well, not literally, but the metaphors work.

You must position your enterprise to catch the waves (Disruptions), navigate those waves when they break (Tipping Points), and use the power of those waves to ride your metaphorical surfboard into the future (Paradigm Shifts).

Seeing around corners and surfing the waves are the two pillars of Insightful Leadership, the kind of leadership that innovates to meet customers' needs, wants, and desires that often change quicker than the weather—or the waves.

Seeing around corners involves anticipating and understanding Disruptions and how multiple Disruptions work together to reach a Tipping Point where the paradigms of the past shift to create a new reality. Insightful Leaders will find opportunities to harness the power (surf) of that Paradigm Shift to innovate through Disruptions.

Insightful Leadership is not magic. It's not a vision from heaven. It's not predicting the future. Insightful Leadership is more akin to a guru sitting on a remote mountaintop spending decades pondering existence. Though, instead of isolating yourself from the world, you are in the world, paying attention to the trends, political changes, legal landscape, and technology changes, especially those outside the scope of your immediate sector or specialty.

For as Disruption creates Tipping Points and Paradigm Shifts, Disruption also creates opportunity. The previous crisis to end all crises, the 2007-2008 financial meltdown, is a perfect example. The Great Recession sparked a flurry of entrepreneurship. By the time it was over, new enterprises like Airbnb, Uber, and Square allowed consumers to conduct business that was impossible when the iPhone was first launched in 2007.[5] If Disruption and opportunity are two sides of the same coin, and Disruption creates opportunity, and we are in an era of perpetual Disruption, then the future of business is also the future of unlimited opportunity for Insightful Leaders.

It will not be survival of the biggest nor survival of the best established. Instead, it will be survival of those most adaptable to their specific environment, as Professor Leon C. Megginson of Louisiana State University wrote in 1963:

"According to Darwin's *Origin of Species*, it is not the most intellectual of the species that survives; it is not the strongest that survives; but the species that survives is the one that is able best to adapt and adjust to the changing environment in which it finds itself."[6]

To survive, species (organizations) must adapt and work cooperatively against common threats to achieve successes they never thought possible. The more things change, the more we need to innovate in response to these changes. A lack of active response will threaten the existence of the organization. A key leadership responsibility, then, is adapting to change and working to overcome Disruptions via innovations. For the sake of anticipating new Disruptions, leaders must have insight.

In this context, the term insight means an understanding of how paradigms will shift based on current Disruptions and Tipping Points. Your goal from insight is to see future Paradigm Shifts and best understand them so you can gain a competitive advantage and surf past your competition.

These days, the explosion of big data gives leaders much more knowledge than in decades past. Without a methodology, however, they often struggle to turn information into intelligence, mistaking casual observations with insight. Here is the methodology I have used for years to build multiple successful companies and, more importantly, continue innovating once the enterprises are surfing the waves of success.

Gaining insights

- Environmental scan: identify Disruptions and understand their impacts (peering around corners).
- Developing insight: anticipate Tipping Points and envision Paradigm Shifts by studying the Disruptions.
- Documenting insight: specify shifts in the future of business that provide opportunities for competitive advantage.

Harnessing the power of insights

- Define obsolete paradigms: identify specific paradigms which, due to Disruptions and Tipping Points, are no longer correct.
- Develop a strategy to replace obsolete paradigms: identify innovations that will replace obsolete paradigms.

Creating success from Insightful Leadership

- Communicate: widely communicate your insights, strategy, and innovations across your organization to harness the power of your insights.
- Achieve alignment: help the organization grasp the shifts of paradigms and how deploying these developed insights will result in a strong competitive advantage in the marketplace.
- Deploy insights: disrupt the status quo and ride your insights to competitive advantage and major success.

Insights are not eureka moments that predict the future. They are an ongoing process of deeply understanding current events and existing paradigms, all based on an in-depth knowledge and understanding of the background of Disruptions, Tipping Points, and Paradigm Shifts.

True insights are the cornerstones of the innovative process. They help us make sense out of Disruptions and Tipping Points, see new emerging underlying truths, or reveal previously unseen truths. Insights can also be a penetrating observation or discovery about unseen truths or an unrecognized fundamental truth that reveals the inner nature of a given situation.

Insights are clear statements that explain shifts in paradigms, thus revealing an opportunity for innovation, or an opportunity to create value.

The Leadership/Management Conundrum

The science and practice of management is in its infancy compared to the history of leadership. Nevertheless, as organizational complexity has grown over the last 100 years, the focus has been on management, not leadership.

Many have gotten into a management-versus-leadership battle. Let us not fall prey to such. The clear fact is, just as a good football team needs a good offense and defense, a good organization requires good management and good leadership.

The challenge, then, lies not in management versus leadership, but rather when leadership should rule and when management should rule. Or, more specifically for this "insightful" discussion, should we be talking about:

1. Insightful Leadership and Management,
2. Insightful Leadership, or
3. Insightful Management?

To answer this question, let's reflect on the meanings of the words *management* and *leadership*.

By definition, management, a noun, consists of a group of people who achieve orderly results by controlling schedules and budgets. Managers plan, organize, direct, and control. They have subordinates who execute plans on a day-to-day basis to accomplish goals, and they have historically been tasked with optimizing those daily operations to produce optimal results. In addition, managers have a circle of power to whom they ask questions about "how" and "when."

Although leadership is also technically a noun, most business officials refer to leadership as a verb. If leadership is not a verb in your business or entrepreneurship world, you need to make it so, or your organization will be left behind.

Leaders communicate, motivate, inspire, and provide guidance. Leaders have followers who are looking across the horizon into the future to embrace Disruptions. Leaders challenge the status quo and guide the development of new strategies. Leaders have a circle of influence to whom they ask questions about "what" and "why."

Consider the following to see the differences between leadership and management:

Leadership

- Visionary
- Innovation
- Long-term change
- Know where they are going
- Servant of the people
- Broad focus on the horizon
- Obtain organizational alignment
- People doing the right things

Management

- Execution
- Administration
- Short-term control
- Know where they are
- Boss of the people
- Narrow focus on the bottom line
- Organizing and staffing
- People doing it right

Leadership is about the future; management is about the present.[7]

Given the definitions of leadership and management and the fact that each tackles different aspects of organizational performance, today's business world clearly has a huge imbalance between management and leadership. Namely, an abundance of management and a shortage of leadership. In today's world where the pandemic still influences our actions, we need much stronger leadership that understands Disruptions, Tipping Points, and Paradigm Shifts. This Insightful Leadership not only looks toward the future instead of back at the past but also examines how to reinvent an organization as it approaches the next wave—all while maintaining or improving the existing wave. This is a prerequisite for organizational success.

Although numbers certainly play a part, Insightful Leadership is more than looking at numbers.

Take predictive analytics, for example. Predictive analytics is an area of statistics that deals with extracting information from data and using it to predict the future. Businesspeople use predictive analytics to identify patterns found in historical data to predict the future. Predictive analytics has real value if the future is an extension of the past.

But Disruption, by definition, is not an extension of the past. Since the business landscape you face will consist of perpetual Disruption, the value of predictive analytics will decline, as predicting the future becomes ever more impossible.

Likewise, scenario planning has value for business people. Scenario planning is a strategic planning process that tests how important "drivers," or known factors that impact business, affect the future. Scenario planning helps in understanding their impact so management can develop long-range plans that are agile enough to deal with how the business landscape unfolds, whether performance is optimistic, normal, or pessimistic.

So, if scenario planning identifies three important drivers, such as deciding on an acquisition, deciding to divest a product offering, or adding a new product line, and if you're looking at optimistic, normal, and pessimistic scenarios, then you're aiming to understand nine potential scenarios, from the ultimate optimist (optimist on all three drivers) to the ultimate pessimist (pessimist on all three drivers). Scenario planning is not about predicting the future; rather, it's about applying one's insights to a few important drivers to better understand the future.

On the other hand, contingency planning is like scenario planning in that "what if" types of questions are being asked, but it only considers one driver, thus ignoring their interactions. Contingency planning is more of a sensitivity analysis.

Scenario planning success is tied to selecting and understanding the right drivers, such as industrial, political, technological, legal, and societal trends that have an impact on the organization, an impact that you can anticipate.

Herein lies the difference between scenario planning and Insightful Leadership. Scenario planning is about anticipating the impacts of drivers. In contrast, Insightful Leadership is not about drivers, but about understanding the Disruptions to business and being able to have insights into how these

Disruptions will cause Tipping Points, resulting in Paradigm Shifts.

Drivers are known factors that impact business while Disruptions are unknown factors that impact business. For over fifty years, scenario planning has had significant value. However, today, where Disruption is the new normal, our efforts must turn from scenario planning to Insightful Leadership.

Insightful Leadership, not more management, is what the future needs, as Insightful Leadership allows us to see around corners and surf the waves of these turbulent times.

Just because you cannot predict the future does not mean you should not try to study trends, Disruptions, Tipping Points, and Paradigm Shifts to gain an understanding of how markets, consumers, and competitors will respond. In fact, perpetual Disruption makes it more important than ever for leaders to understand and glean insights about how they can upgrade their strategy and performance to earn favor with their customers, driving competitive advantage.

The best in business seem to be able to see and comprehend things other mere mortals cannot. Many business writers define seeing around corners as the ability to anticipate problems before they happen. The meaning of the phrase "seeing around corners" is more specific than just anticipating problems. I define "seeing around corners" as the ability to observe and understand Disruptions and anticipate Tipping Points, therefore allowing organizations to pivot when (or even before) paradigms shift.

This goes beyond the traditional industrial engineering precept of optimizing all operations. It is impossible to optimize everything in the face of constant Disruption. By the time you implement optimal solutions, circumstances will change, the optimal will no longer be optimal, and you will have to return to the drawing board.

Even before the Disruptions of 2020-2022, I have been recommending that enterprises pursue optionality, not optimality. In the post-pandemic era, generating options will require using more than your five senses of taste, touch, smell, sight, and hearing. You must add insight as your sixth sense, a sense gleaned from hard work.

Gifted people who seem able to predict the future simply spend more time thinking outside-in, questioning potential changes and asking, "what if?" Instead of being surprised, they have options ready. They know they cannot control external events, and instead of generating options after events happen, they're ready to respond quickly.[8]

Learning, for them, is an action sport that goes beyond school, formal classes, practice problems, and risk-free iterations. Crazy ideas, to them, are not so crazy. They know business can go beyond dollars and cents, often acting on visions that change the world to make it a better place. Often, that better place comes with making bold decisions that fly in the face of conventional market research.[9]

And yes, this can involve killing the cash cow, as Steve Jobs did when transitioning from the iPod to the iPhone and iPad.[10]

Imagine where Kodak would be if it had embraced digital photography and captured a percentage of the mobile phone camera market. Instead, they chose not to shift their paradigm but rather to maintain their dominance in film. When's the last time you bought 35mm film?

While Kodak lost money on each digital camera it sold, Fujifilm diversified, adapting its technologies for pharmaceuticals, cosmetics, and the soon-to-be ubiquitous LCD panels. When digital killed the cash cow of film, Fujifilm was ready to remain profitable.[11]

Instead of trying to predict the future, you should measure your success by whether your enterprise even considered what happened as a possibility and prepared accordingly —optionality.[12]

These options will help you innovate through Disruptions.

Think back to the Great Recession mentioned above. Innovations came from startups with nothing to lose—the Ubers and Airbnbs.

In fact, only 9% of established companies emerged stronger from the Great Recession while 17% went bankrupt. That 9% emerged stronger by increasing operational efficiencies to reduce costs while investing in the future by spending on marketing, R&D, and new assets.[13] This is innovating through Disruption. This is surfing the waves of today's turbulent world.

With Disruption as the new normal, established companies that remain successful and continue growing look for the new instead of doubling down on the old. Insightful Leaders will be the ones who identify and pursue the right investments, grasping innovation for entrepreneurial gain.

Insightful Leadership will dictate the difference between great performance and weak performance. Insightful Leadership is the mantra of leaders living in times of perpetual Disruption.

You, the entrepreneur, business leader, or organizational leader will have to spend time examining criteria far beyond the scope of the drivers in scenario planning or numbers yielded by predictive analytics.

You must be aware of things you're not thinking about right now. If I told you in 2008 that a major transportation company wouldn't own fleets of vehicles (Uber) and a major lodging company wouldn't own any rooms (Airbnb), would you have believed me?

I, for example, have over four decades of experience in industrial engineering and supply chains. But I, like many others, need to spend time on things outside my comfort zone that disrupt my world, change my paradigms, and force me to rethink how to achieve excellence and competitive advantage.

Today, Insightful Leadership is the battle cry of business success. Insightful Leadership will have your organization riding the wave into the future.

Why Insightful Leadership Now?

Insightful Leadership is in stark contrast to visionary leadership, the hallmark of business for decades. For years, leaders have articulated a vision and worked to align their organization's execution with that vision. In eras where Disruption was minimal compared to today, that worked. Organizations could go years or even decades doing what they did, traveling from the valley, climbing to the peak of achievement, settling in on a plateau of success. Mild Disruptions did not force changes in vision.

In our modern world, however, enterprises must continuously reinvent. Aligning your organization around a static vision will prevent you from responding to the new normal of Disruption.

There is no resting on the peak of a mountaintop. There is no solid shoreline whatsoever. In our turbulent world, your enterprise must surf wave to wave to wave to wave. If you think you can rest onshore, your business is truly doomed. If you rest, your organization will drown. You must prepare to catch the next wave even before your current wave plays out. Once the wave you're riding ends, it's already too late.

Do not wait until it is too late. Embrace Insightful Leadership now.

---

1. Leonhardt, Megan. "COVID isn't the thing keeping people working from home anymore." *Fortune*, 1 Apr. 2022, fortune.com/2022/04/01/remote-work-from-home-march-jobs-report-covid/.
2. Gladwell, Malcolm. *The Tipping Point: How Little Things Can Make a Big Difference*. Little, Brown and Company, 2000.
3. Stevens, Pippa. "The Ship That Blocked the Suez Canal May Be Free, but Experts Warn the Supply Chain Impact Could Last Months." *CNBC*, 29 Mar. 2021, www.cnbc.com/2021/03/29/suez-canal-is-moving-but-the-supply-chain-impact-could-last-months.html.
4. "Japanese Carmakers Assess Impact of Fire At Renesas Chip Plant." *Reuters*, 22 Mar. 2021, www.reuters.com/business/autos-transportation/japan-car-makers-scramble-assess-impact-renesas-auto-chip-plant-fire-2021-03-22/.

5. Halkett, Richard. "Innovating Through Disruption." *AWS*, aws.amazon. com/executive-insights/analysts/innovating-through-disruption/. Accessed July 26, 2022.
6. Megginson, Leon C. "Lessons from Europe for American Business." *Southwestern Social Science Quarterly,* vol. 44, no. 1, 1963, pp. 3-13. University of Cambridge, www.darwinproject.ac.uk/people/about-darwin/six-things-darwin-never-said/evolution-misquotation.
7. Barker, Joel. "CFBusinessForum - Joel Barker - The Importance of Paradigms in the 21st Century." *YouTube,* uploaded by challengefuture, 13 Apr. 2012, www.youtube.com/watch?v=wOXWSg_PyTQ.
8. Bradt, George. "The Secret to Seeing Around Corners." *Forbes,* 14 Jan. 2020, www.forbes.com/sites/georgebradt/2020/01/14/the-secret-to-seeing-around-corners/?sh=654280ad666f.
9. Zwilling, Martin. "Entrepreneurs Who Can See Around the Corner." *BusinessInsider,* 20 July 2012, www.businessinsider.com/entrepreneurs-who-can-see-around-the-corner-2012-7.
10. Zwilling, Martin. "Entrepreneurs Who Can See Around the Corner." *Insider,* 20 July 2012, https://www.businessinsider.com/entrepreneurs-who-can-see-around-the-corner-2012-7.
11. Kmia, Oliver. "Why Kodak Died and Fujifilm Thrived: A Tale of Two Film Companies." *PetaPixel,* 19 Oct. 2018, www.petapixel.com/2018/10/19/why-kodak-died-and-fujifilm-thrived-a-tale-of-two-film-companies.
12. McGrath, Rita. "What Does it Mean to 'See Around Corners?'" *YouTube,* uploaded by Ecosystems Services, 30 Mar. 2020, www.youtube.com/watch?v=ktdk6EWW3IU.
13. Halkett, Richard. "Innovating Through Disruption." *AWS*, 1999, aws. amazon.com/executive-insights/analysts/innovating-through-disruption/.

2 PREMONITIONS FROM THE PAST —THE BLACK SWAN AND VUCA

Nassim Nicholas Taleb's 2007 book *The Black Swan: The Impact of the Highly Improbable* co-opted the term "Black Swan" to describe unpredictable, rare, or catastrophic events. Some examples include the rise of the internet, Hurricane Katrina, and the September 11 attacks on the World Trade Center and Pentagon. The U.S. Army War College coined the acronym VUCA (volatility, uncertainty, complexity, and ambiguity) to describe the post-Cold War world. These concepts, Black Swans and VUCA, both help describe an onslaught of random, unpredictable events.

The Black Swan of 2020, the global COVID-19 pandemic, combined with years of digital innovation and ongoing geopolitical and financial crises, have taken the world of business beyond VUCA into perpetual Disruption.

I spent much of my career immersed in largely predictable and measurable processes, like the material handling and logistics I taught students at North Carolina State University or, after branching into consulting, the networks of warehouses and transportation processes I designed and constructed for clients.

As my business grew, I moved my research into entrepreneurship and leadership. However, quantifying leadership was a bit more difficult; good leadership, unlike a solid material handling system, was harder to replicate.

That's why Taleb's *The Black Swan: The Impact of the Highly Improbable* struck me like lightning.[1] Taleb took his term from the fact that, for centuries, the scientific world thought all swans were white... until 1697 when a Dutch explorer discovered black swans in Australia.

While that first-known physical Black Swan upended the zoological study of birds, Taleb co-opts the term as his metaphor for how history, including our world of business and entrepreneurship, is dominated by catastrophic, rare, and unpredictable events.

The former trader turned researcher and author classifies most major scientific discoveries and historic events as Black Swans, undirected and unpredicted. For Taleb, a Black Swan shares three characteristics: it is an outlier because nothing in the past can convincingly point to its possibility, it carries an extreme impact, and humans "concoct explanations for its occurrence after the fact, making it explainable and predictable."

Taleb points out that nobody foresaw the rise of the internet, the personal computer, the dissolution of the Soviet Union, or World War I. In fact, when the great European powers faced off in 1914, many predicted a short fight. Penicillin was discovered via an accidentally contaminated staphylococcus culture plate. Scientists discovered Viagra while searching for a cardiovascular drug to lower blood pressure.

Taleb also stated that "the future will be increasingly less predictable, while both human nature and social 'science' seem to conspire to hide the idea from us."

And bam—Taleb's theory dovetailed with my real-life business experience in the years immediately before Taleb's book but particularly as the business world unfolded in the years since *The Black Swan*'s publication.

And that Disruption, or VUCA, has been your world, too.

Prior to the fall of the Soviet Union, the U.S. Army War College coined the acronym VUCA (volatility, uncertainty, complexity and ambiguity) to describe what they expected in the post-Cold War world.

Volatility is the nature and frequency of change. The marketplace changes faster than companies can generate adequate responses.

Uncertainty is the impossibility of accurately predicting the future or defining standard operating requirements that will last. We are living in the most uncertain times in the history of the world.

Complexity is the confusion that arises from the lack of clear distinctions between retailers, distributors, manufacturers, and wholesalers. As an example, while grocery store private labels have been around forever, consumer packaged goods (CPG) companies are now creating their own eCommerce sites and selling direct-to-consumer (D2C). With the rise of digitalization, companies must sell everywhere.

Ambiguity describes the inability to understand what is really going to happen. The digital age is paving the way for new products, services, and business models. With ambiguity, it's less clear what will be successful enough to survive on the market. It's the result of the haziness of reality.

You know this VUCA exists even if you don't care to admit it. Technological progress (including the Black Swans of the internet and the rise of the computer), as well as wars and other geopolitical events have led to increasing levels of VUCA in the business world throughout the second decade of the 21st century.

China's manufacturing sector has exploded, making it the factory of the world. International trade has skyrocketed.

Biotechnology has developed life-saving devices, from the mRNA vaccines fighting COVID-19 to initial success with 3D-printed human organs and more.[2]

Apple's iPhone transformed our lifestyles, fitting into our pockets a mobile communications device more powerful than the rooms of computers the Apollo missions used to put men on the moon and bring them back home to Earth. Never-before-seen Twitter storms often dominate our politics, and we use our phones (small computers, really) not only to call out political opponents on social media but also to communicate with friends, family, and business associates. Apps like Spotify, Netflix, and Airbnb have also changed how we interact with the music, film, and hotel industries forever.

With Amazon, we started clicking and waiting instead of driving to the store and hauling our purchases home. We started talking to our devices through voice activation technology, viewing virtual and augmented reality through wearable technology, and telling time by looking at our smartwatches (or they can tell you the time by speaking to you).

More of us are driving our electric and hybrid cars, as Tesla has grown from producing zero cars to becoming the world's most valuable automotive company, spawning startups like Rivian, Lucid Motors, and several others.

Artificial intelligence and machine learning moved from the realm of science fiction to the business boardroom and our homes (like with Alexa and Siri). Instead of buying packets of software to install on our increasingly powerful and smaller computers, we operate in the cloud.

Even the weather has been growing more unpredictable: the snows are worse, the summers are hotter, the hurricanes are increasing, and the typhoons are growing stronger.

This is why your five-year plan was already out of date before July. That logistics network you expected to handle demand for the next four years operated at capacity by year two (or, even worse, operated at a lower capacity than you expected). The material handling system that had the highest

ROI two years ago is woefully inadequate because the labor needed to operate at the highest ROI is not available. That customer requirement forecast for clothing that works so well will become useless as more customers permanently transition to working from home, buying fewer dress shirts and more T-shirts.

That's why, even before COVID-19 and the Disruptions of the last few years roiled the waves of our manufacturing and supply chain world, I started recommending that clients pursue optionality instead of optimality, especially in their supply chain operations. Industrial engineers design systems for the most efficient, cost-effective operations—optimality. But once locked into the optimal, some systems, like the Titanic facing the iceberg, are rather hard to turn in another direction.

Business leadership before the current era can be likened to the differences between quarterbacking a football team of eight year olds versus playing quarterback in big-time college football. The eight year old hands the ball to Mark, the biggest kid on the team. Sometimes he'll hand it off to Joe, the fastest kid on the team. While you may view your eight year old as a future Patrick Mahomes, he's not standing behind center and audibling to another play. Eight-year-old footballers concentrate on optimality—the biggest and fastest, or a combination of both.

While Trevor Lawrence at age eight simply handed the ball off, he was leading the Clemson Tigers to a college national football championship by age nineteen, reading defenses and sometimes changing plans just before the snap. Increasingly in high-level high school football and definitely by college and the NFL, football becomes a game of optionality. Both sports and leadership require adaptability.

As I discussed in my June 2019 YouTube video "Anti-Brittle: Succeeding and Flourishing in these Uncertain and Volatile Times," optionality will defeat optimality in times of volatility, uncertainty, complexity, and ambiguity.

Despite comments by some who viewed that video after the pandemic struck, my video, of course, was not a prediction of COVID-19, the mother of the mother of the mother of all Disruptions. In fact, nobody predicted such a thing. If you examine the business press in January 2020, the top ten most feared Disruptions for what became the year of the pandemic did not even mention a pandemic, even though the first COVID-19 news reports had already surfaced in China. Then, the Black Swan of COVID-19 struck, making options even more important.

The fact that we had a worldwide pandemic did not in and of itself make COVID-19 a Black Swan. Many people warned that the world was vulnerable to such an event. Remember, however, that Taleb spends a lot of time discussing how Black Swans differ based on viewpoint. Thanksgiving is a Black Swan for the turkey, not the farmer. COVID-19's impacts made many in the business world, even those whose companies survived, feel like the Thanksgiving Day turkey.

In the world of business leadership, entrepreneurship, supply chain, and manufacturing—the world I and my readers inhabit—the *when* is often just as important as the *what*. And, like many Black Swans and Disruptions in a world of perpetual Disruption, nobody predicted that COVID-19 would shut down much of the world by March 2020 with intermittent starts, stops, and worries continuing for years.

Even after the spring 2020 lockdowns, many thought COVID-19 would dissipate by summer. But for two years, every time a new variant raises its head, the specter of more Disruptions rises.

Clearly, not many people "peered around the corners" to anticipate COVID-19's magnitude and its continual impact on everyone, everywhere, and everything.

Beyond the human toll—the sickness, deaths, and misery —historians will remember COVID-19 as the Disruption that changed how we live, work, shop, learn, and go about our daily lives. In other words, everything businesses are built to serve.

COVID-19 is like discovering not just a Black Swan in Australia but a Black Swan ten times the size of all previous known swans—something more akin to a prehistoric giant pterodactyl, not a modern bird. From the viewpoint of our business world, COVID-19 is the mother of the mother of the mother of all Disruptions, the defining Black Swan of our era.

The scope of COVID-19's impact delineates a difference between how Taleb and I approach the term. His book is about discrete events, and Black Swans are a subject. For me, you, and other business leaders and entrepreneurs, Black Swans are a phase that leads to something else, a part of the Disruption-Tipping Point-Paradigm Shift process we must go through to develop the insights that will allow us to stay ahead of the competition, or at least survive to surf another day.

For us, Disruptions are sometimes Black Swans. Sometimes, however, Disruptions simply come from VUCA. Both types of Disruptions can lead to deep insights into whether a Tipping Point is on the way, but the fact of the matter is that insights are more obvious during a Black Swan event than with simple Disruptions, even in a world where Disruption is the new normal.

The important thing is not any one Disruption or any one Black Swan but the learning you can glean from what will change about how businesses must serve their future customers.

The Black Swan of COVID-19 caused governments to lock down entire countries, and many people transitioned into working from home. The previous decades worth of digital innovation allowed those people to shop via a computer click instead of taking a trip to the store, skyrocketing eCommerce sales. Work from home, exploding eCommerce, and geopolitical/financial crises broke the supply chains the world used to serve those customers.

And since then, the world has suffered from a wealth of non-Black Swan Disruptions.

Some Disruptions, such as when U.S. business bankruptcies hit their highest level in a decade in 2020 or when massive semiconductor shortages affected businesses everywhere, were obviously related to the COVID-19 Black Swan.

But many others were not, and some only had localized effects. If you were in their crosshairs as an Insightful Leader, though, you had to handle their aftereffects.

The North Atlantic faced down a record-breaking thirty named storms in 2020. Of the fourteen hurricanes and seven major hurricanes, eleven named storms struck the U.S. coastline,[3] and California alone suffered through five of the state's largest wildfires ever.[4] In 2020, a port exploded in Beirut. In 2021, a condo collapsed in Miami. Also in 2021, a container ship got stuck in the Suez Canal, shutting down that major shipping artery for nearly a week.

Sparked by the changing climate, billions of locusts struck parts of Africa throughout 2019-2021 with a severity not seen in decades (on a note related to this book's prescription for dealing with Black Swans and Disruption, a concerted effort using apps, machine learning, artificial intelligence, and crowdsourcing protected $1.5 billion worth of agricultural products from the locust swarms, "saving the livelihoods of 34 million people.").[5]

Before the Disruptions of the last few years, many companies had transitioned to a China + 1 strategy of adding Vietnam, Cambodia, and others to their global supply chains. Unfortunately, many of those countries lack adequate port facilities, creating backlogs and other problems; it's an option still in transition. Beyond that, there's continual social upheaval related to race in the United States and, internationally, human rights. These are all Disruptions, though, not Black Swans.

After all, wildfires in discrete geographic locations don't affect the entire globe. A hurricane that tears through Florida does not affect people in Idaho. The billions of locusts in Africa certainly harm those living (or starving) through the devastation, not those safely ensconced in Northern Europe. The Port of Beirut explosion was devastating locally, killing hundreds, injuring thousands, and leaving hundreds of thousands homeless.

But beyond volunteers, donors, and others engaged in relief efforts, none of those Disruptions affected manufacturing in Shanghai, transoceanic shipping, or the myriad ways businesses worldwide source, produce, and deliver goods and services.

Depending on future events, some issues could swirl into Tipping Points that will later gush into Paradigm Shifts or a devastating Black Swan if, say, a shooting war erupts between China and Taiwan.

And who knows what the results will be from Russia's second invasion of Ukraine in less than a decade? The former Soviet Union is a major supplier of fertilizer, and those prices are skyrocketing. In addition to fertilizer, what are the impacts of the invasion on other critical commodities such as wheat, barley, corn, potatoes, aluminum, iron, nickel, palladium, titanium, mercury, manganese, uranium, ammonia, neon, and more?

Of course, that means opportunity elsewhere. Perhaps mining firms in other locales can step into the breach. In Africa, for example, the continent's richest man just opened a massive fertilizer plant in Nigeria.[6]

From dealing with on-again off-again government-mandated business shutdowns to unemployment to GDP fluctuations to significant performance issues to geopolitical upheaval to significant inflation for the first time this millennia, this is the most dynamic, uncertain time we have ever witnessed. The great state of VUCA that the last few years has wrought will require multiple responses—options—from Insightful Leaders.

The animal world provides an appropriate metaphor.

Ants are what biologists call ametabolous: a baby ant grows into an adult ant, but it otherwise undergoes little or no metamorphosis. Ants, in the world of business, represent continuous improvement—the Lean Six Sigma programs, plan-do-check-act, etc.

Baby grasshoppers, on the other hand, which start with no wings or reproductive organs, develop later. Their partial metamorphosis is labeled hemimetaboly, akin to business transformation.

Caterpillars, of course, go through total transformation on their way to butterfly status.

Can you imagine being a caterpillar? You are a dust-sucking worm who drags your belly around in the dirt, and one night, you tire and fall asleep. When you wake up in the morning, it's still dark out. Then, you realize it's dark because you're wrapped in a cocoon.

What the heck is going on here? you wonder. *Why am I in this cocoon?* And so you eat your way out of the cocoon, and when the light comes in you look down and, son of a gun, you have wings.

You have gone through a total metamorphosis, what biologists call holometabolism. You are reinvented.

This represents business reinvention, necessary in a world of continual disruption and unpredictable, devastating Black Swans.

As shown in Figure 2.1, depending upon the depth and severity of the Disruption, an organization's circle of life will require ant-like continuous improvement, grasshopper-like transformation, and caterpillar-like reinvention, and you likely will be in some phase of all three most of the time. Only Black Swans require total reinvention from the caterpillar to the butterfly. Only through Insightful Leadership can you transform Black Swan situations into butterflies.

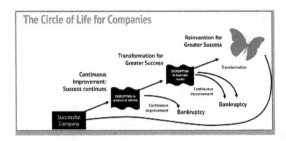

Figure 2.1

As Taleb wrote, history has been dominated by unpredictable, random events. Your business' future will be dominated by them, too. Therefore, you must develop systems and solutions that are agile and resilient: optionality. Insightful Leaders will have to deal with these unpredictable Disruptions as they are, not as they wish they were. The key to success is playing the hand you were dealt like it was the hand that you wanted.

Despite the fact that many have declared the pandemic over, COVID-19 will forever remain in our minds, just as the Great Depression did for the people who lived through it. How we respond to these difficult times will impact the rest of our lives.

For the proper response, you will need to anticipate which Disruptions generate Tipping Points—and which do not.

1. Taleb, Nicholas Nassim. *The Black Swan: The Impact of the Highly Improbable*. Random House Trade Paperbacks, 2010.
2. Lord, Brian. "Bladder Grown From 3d Bioprinted Tissue Continues to Function After 14 Years." *3D Printing Industry*, 12 Sept. 2018, 3dprintingindustry.com/news/bladder-grown-from-3d-bioprinted-tissue-continues-to-function-after-14-years-139631/
3. "Record-Breaking Atlantic Hurricane Season Draws to an End." *National Oceanic and Atmospheric Administration*. 10 June 2021, www.noaa.gov/media-release/record-breaking-atlantic-hurricane-season-draws-to-end.
4. "Top 20 Largest California Wildfires." *The California Department of Forestry and Fire Protection*. 13 Jan. 2022, www.fire.ca.gov/media/4jandlhh/top20_acres.pdf.

5. Nuwer, Rachel. "As Locusts Swarmed East Africa, This Tech Helped Squash Them." *The New York Times*, 8 Apr. 2021, www.nytimes.com/2021/04/08/science/locust-swarms-africa.html.
6. Tan, Huileng. "The Richest Man in Africa Just Opened the Continent's Biggest Fertilizer Plant." *Yahoo Finance*, 24 Mar. 2022, finance.yahoo.com/news/richest-man-africa-just-opened-073543130.html.

3 TIPPING POINTS: WHEN LITTLE THINGS MEAN A LOT

In *The Tipping Point: How Little Things Can Make a Big Difference*, Canadian journalist Malcolm Gladwell writes that "ideas and products and messages and behaviors spread like viruses do." So do Disruptions. Many Disruptions come and go, causing no more than a ripple in the ocean. In my book *Revolution: Take Charge Strategies for Business Success*, I call these ripples management by fad (MBF) and give examples of employee involvement, organizational development, quality circles, and total quality management. Others, such as the 2001 terrorist attack on the World Trade Center and the Pentagon or the invention of the internet, change the world.

Could a few dozen hipsters and a pair of Manhattan fashion designers, without trying, resurrect an almost terminally uncool brand of casual shoes?

Could one horseman's midnight ride spark a battle that presages revolutions worldwide?

Could cracking down on farebeating, aggressive panhandling, and subway graffiti plummet violent crime levels in a major metropolitan area?

Why yes, says journalist and author Malcolm Gladwell. His 2000 bestseller *The Tipping Point: How Little Things Can Make a Big Difference* marshals an impressive body of evidence from sociology, criminology, marketing, and history to make the case that ideas, products, messages, and behaviors spread like diseases.[1] As such, they grow from small changes into critical masses, becoming Tipping Points that trigger an epidemic.

Small changes could include things like working from home, ordering more products online, and redirecting your funds from vacations and experiences to manufactured goods — exactly how life changed during COVID-19.

For Gladwell, life is a series of epidemics—crime rates, measles outbreaks, fashion trends, historical events, etc.— where results are often disproportionate to the size of their causes. His three rules of epidemics are 1) The Law of the Few, 2) The Stickiness Factor, and 3) The Power of Context. For Gladwell, epidemics are a function of people who transmit infectious agents, the infectious agent itself, and the environment where the infectious agent operates.

In his book's first example, Gladwell relates how, by the mid 1990s, Hush Puppies' shoe sales had slowed to the point that parent company Wolverine considered wiping out the brand. Then, word got out that the Manhattan nightclub scene favored the decidedly unglamorous shoes. They became so popular that two New York fashion designers featured the brushed-suede shoes in their collections and fashion shows.

For Gladwell, this circumstance embodies the Law of the Few, where a small coterie of people transmits a trend to the masses. Manhattan hipsters transmitted formerly stodgy Hush Puppies to the eyes of key designers. This virus of cool-ness spread from the designers into the general population, and Hush Puppies went from moribund to a Tipping Point to a smash hit, with sales mushrooming from about 30,000 a year to more than 1.5 million.

Gladwell's three rules of epidemics don't only apply to the present. On April 18, 1775, Paul Revere had a cool message: British regular troops were marching out from Boston to seize guns and munitions from Massachusetts militias. Revere and the less-remembered William Dawes (more on Dawes later) spread the word around the countryside. The militia prepared, grabbing their muskets, powder, and ammunition before the British could confiscate them, and the battles of Lexington and Concord triggered the American Revolution.

Revere's message stuck (The Stickiness Factor). Gladwell speculates that if Revere's midnight message had involved a sale on pewter mugs at the Bostonian's silversmith shop, the ride would be ... less memorable, to put it lightly. Gladwell defines stickiness as the quality a message needs to be successful: Are those shoes really that comfortable and, in a retro way, kind of stylish when paired with a blazer and black jeans at the Manhattan nightclub? Are the British regulars really coming?

Context matters, too. Revere rode into an area hot with ferment after years of revolutionary agitation by American colonists who favored a break with Great Britain. If he had galloped from, say, Sunbury-on-Thames to London warning of British regulars, his audience would have been less than receptive.

Later, Gladwell illustrates the Power of Context with his tale of crime-fighting in New York where, once again, little things—not Batman and his cool gadgets—made a difference in the lives of innocent Gotham City civilians.

In the 1980s, New York crime was epidemic, both underground in the subway system and on the Big Apple's streets. Graffiti littered the subway, neighborhoods were filled with broken windows, squeegee men demanded money for cleaning off car windshields in traffic (often with the implicit threat of violence to nonpayers), and thousands of people a day jumped turnstiles to avoid paying the $1 subway fare.

According to the broken windows theory of policing, decrepit and rundown areas act as a petri dish for crime. As Gladwell relates, if nothing is done about one broken window, broken windows proliferate, society assumes no one is in charge, and no one cares. As residents conclude that anything goes, more quality-of-life crimes lead to an increase in violent crime—the muggings, beatings, rapes, and murders.

With this in mind, the New York Transit Authority prioritized ending graffiti and farebeating. A significant minority of the people jumping turnstiles or otherwise avoiding paying subway fares had outstanding warrants, previous arrests, or weapons. The relentless cleanup led would-be criminals to conclude that they had best leave their weapons at home—and fork over a buck.

The yearslong campaign worked, Gladwell wrote. Subway crime—from $1 farebeating to more violent actions— declined precipitously. New York City officials moved the battle aboveground in the mid 1990s, targeting aggressive panhandling, public drunkenness and urination, and minor property damage among other quality-of-life crimes.

Just like it had in the subterranean passages of the city, New York's overall crime rate plunged. Gladwell and other proponents of the broken windows theory maintain that the change in environment, or the Power of Context, led to a Tipping Point that reversed the crime epidemic.

Those three rules of epidemics (the Law of the Few, the Stickiness Factor, and the Power of Context) also require Gladwell's three agents of infection: connectors, mavens, and salesmen.

Gladwell characterizes Revere as a maven, or an information specialist. They're the ones who know the best table at each restaurant, the best place to buy your Christmas ham, and when supermarkets' "extra low prices" are really lower prices instead of the regular everyday price with a marketing sticker stuck on the product.

Mavens tell people about what they know. Because mavens are knowledgeable and trusted, their word goes a long way toward convincing others.

If a maven recommends a vacation resort, you will likely book a stay. You and your family will have a fantastic time, and you will recommend it to all your friends, who also will have a fantastic sojourn. And none of you, including the maven, gets a commission.

Revere also was a connector, a person with large networks that span many different areas of life. Gladwell quotes from David Hackett Fischer's book *Paul Revere's Ride*, which describes how the gregarious and social Bostonian did everything from serving on streetlight committees to performing the duties of the county coroner to doing the work of a city health official to founding a fire insurance company and associations that fought poverty. Revere was the kind of guy you would pick to serve as jury foreman—oh yeah, he did that too.

In other words, he was known, and his pre-ride service in the anti-British revolutionary movement positioned him perfectly as a trusted messenger. In industrial engineering/business management terms, I liken connectors to those who can break down the silos between different corporate functions and departments, bringing together sales, planning, procurement, manufacturing, and distribution from within the company. Similarly, outside of the company, all links of the supply chain to the company require a connector to bring the different organizations together to provide the supply of goods to meet the demands of your consumers. Without connectors, infrastructure collapses.

Gladwell contrasts Revere with his partner William Dawes, who also rode around the countryside warning of the Redcoats. His ride was less than successful, and he is barely remembered. Dawes was, in Gladwell's terms, an ordinary man with an ordinary social circle. As Fischer detailed in his book, Dawes would not have known whose doors to knock on in the towns along his route. As a result, he did not awaken the town fathers and militia commanders, and few people responded to his call.

Mavens are data banks with knowledge. Connectors spread that knowledge beyond the maven's networks. Salesmen convince the late adopters. Revere was the trusted maven and connector who sounded the alarm. Salesmen—in this case, militia officers and townspeople who gathered on the green to discuss whether to respond—helped convince the undecided to grab their guns and confront the British troops. And, again, the context of years of agitation against what colonists considered British tyranny made that sales pitch a bit easier.

And although Revere did hope to spark an American Revolution, he likely didn't know that the ideals of liberty enshrined in the Declaration of Independence ("all men are created equal") would trigger global abolitionist, women's suffrage, and political rights movements, from Haiti to France to Ireland in the 1700s to the anti-monarchical 1848 revolutions that swept through Europe.

Gladwell spends much of the book translating his theory into many walks of life, including anti-smoking, gun violence, suicide epidemics, business management, and marketing campaigns. I think *The Tipping Point* perfectly captures what happened worldwide in the first few months after COVID-19 tore out of the Far East in 2020.

It's true that COVID-19 didn't need connectors, mavens, or salesmen; the threat of disease, the fear of death, and the power of government mandates did all the work. COVID-19 was connector, maven, and salesman all in one or, as I'm terming the pandemic, the permanent destroyer of the old ways of doing business, the titanic tidal wave that forced all to bring new surfboards to the seashore.

But a quick environmental scan reveals that just a couple of societal changes (the Law of the Few) accelerated history and transformed the world. Sally started working from home. Jeffrey started buying groceries online. With extra cash from taxpayer-funded stimulus checks and nowhere to go, Ichiro bought a new home theater system instead of that trip to Japan to see his relatives.

You wouldn't think a little thing like ordering groceries online, driving to the store, and having Publix or Safeway workers stuff them in your trunk as you relax in the parking lot would transform the world—until hundreds of millions of people worldwide, triggered by fear of a highly contagious virus, do the same thing.

Then, those little ripples grow to a tsunami overnight, pounding carefully planned, intricate, and worldwide supply chains into the surf. From this, you can determine the type of insight that needs to be developed and documented so you can decide if your supply chain needs a new type of surfboard.

If the lockdowns had nearly eliminated COVID-19 infections and death in a few weeks, perhaps people would have gone back to their old ways by April or May of 2020. But COVID-19 definitely had Gladwell's Stickiness Factor.

As with Gladwell's theory, the context of society matters. Such a worldwide pandemic in, say, 1981—before modern technology, the internet, and eCommerce—would have led to different societal changes. Indeed, COVID-19 accelerated history to where we could have been years ago if businesses and consumers had surfed toward change instead of watching fearfully from the shore. The Black Swan of the rise of the internet and the personal computer made a world of working and shopping from home possible years ago, but society ignored the possibilities.

Managers and leaders stuck with the old paradigms of having employees spend hours getting ready and traveling to work and/or traveling to clients' locations to meet face to face. Much of that could have been done just as well via Zoom or other applications. We enforced dress standards for office and travel to maintain our "professional image." Remember when people actually dressed up to go to work?

We kept believing an employee's value and dedication were somehow demonstrated by the hours they were at work instead of the results they achieved. Bosses believed their employees' work/family balance needed to be monitored to make sure the employees dedicated sufficient time to their jobs.

Now, after the stay-at-home mandates, we look back at ourselves and ask, "What were we thinking?"

So while some Disruptions come and go, COVID-19 and the Disruptions of the last few years will not be like those previous "Disruptions" that I call management by fad (employee involvement, organizational development, quality circles, and total quality management).[2]

Beyond its mortality rates, COVID-19 will be remembered as the virus that changed the world. From its genesis of a few cases in China in late 2019, COVID-19 went from a small ripple in the ocean to triggering multiple tsunamis that upended corporate surfboards across the seven seas.

Rather quickly, and definitely by April 2020, small, society-wide behavioral changes begat the three almost simultaneous Tipping Points identified in this book:

- The lockdown, which sparked the Paradigm Shifts of working from home and changed how we communicate, socialize and interact with each other in business and life.
- The explosion of eCommerce (enabled by digital innovation), which sparked the Paradigm Shift of how we buy goods and services.
- The supply chain failures where—thanks to the lockdowns, eCommerce and geopolitical/financial crises—the broader population and the media realized for the first time how important supply chains are to every

facet of life and shifted the paradigm of how businesses deliver goods.

---

1. Gladwell, Malcolm. *The Tipping Point: How Little Things Can Make a Big Difference*. Little, Brown and Company, 2000.
2. For more on such management by fad, see my book *Revolution: Take Charge Strategies for Business Success*.

4 THE PARADIGM EFFECTS—GOING BEYOND JOEL BARKER'S VISION

In the 1980s, Joel Barker taught us all about paradigms and Paradigm Shifts. Paradigm Shifts are fundamental changes in how things are done. After the great pandemic of 2020, the paradigm about paradigms shifted. The new reality is that Paradigm Shifts are not always triggered by some outsider who is unconstrained by prior thinking, but rather because informed insiders understand that the root causes of Paradigm Shifts come from Disruptions that flow into Tipping Points that create a new reality—a new paradigm. The Paradigm Effect, coined by Barker, is when you gain the right insight into Disruptions, peer around corners to see the Tipping Points forming, and harness the power of those Paradigm Shifts before they occur.

While COVID-19 accelerated history (more on that in Chapter 6), the pandemic also returned me to the past—my library, specifically for Joel Barker's *Discovering the Future: The Business of Paradigms.*[1]

In 1985, Barker introduced me to paradigm thinking, the

idea that human beings view the world through a set of rules and regulations that define our boundaries and tell us how to succeed within those boundaries. Barker defines success as solving problems using the rules of one's paradigm.

When paradigms change, the rules are in flux, and you need to adapt accordingly. Examples of Paradigm Shifts include the Swiss inventing the quartz watch but not deeming it worthy of investment, letting others dominate the market; dozens of companies turning down electrostatic photography (the Xerox machine); and Japan's success adopting W. Edwards Deming's management techniques to become the world's number one quality manufacturer.

In turbulent times, Barker suggests what he calls paradigm pliancy, or seeking new ways to do things, actively challenging your current paradigm. My idea of optionality is key to practicing paradigm pliancy.

Rereading Barker during COVID-19 sparked a eureka moment. I knew that Disruptions led to Tipping Points, but I had not realized that Tipping Points led to Paradigm Shifts.

COVID-19, the disruptor of our lifetime, the destroyer that stopped the factory of the world, the great white shark that swallowed the surfboard of success, combined with other Disruptions (digital innovation, geopolitical and financial crises) to directly wave in the three Tipping Points I discuss in this book: the lockdowns, eCommerce explosion, and broken supply chains.

All three of these Tipping Points are related, and Insightful Leaders will understand and accept the Paradigm Shifts necessary to deal with this new reality. In a world where Disruption is the new normal, entrepreneurs, leaders, and managers peer around corners to gauge which Disruptions will lead to Tipping Points(s) and create new Paradigms. Those are the waves you must ride to entrepreneurial success. This is difficult for humans for two reasons: the velocity of today's shifts and how we relate to Paradigms.

First, Barker's book details paradigms that took decades or

centuries to change, things like scientific disciplines that shifted over four hundred years, or the social acceptability of men sporting long hair, which happened in two decades between the 1960s and the 1980s. Clearly, different paradigms take different amounts of time to shift.

Second, these days, because of constant VUCA accelerated by the pandemic, we are talking about paradigms that shift overnight and then shift again three months later. Let me illustrate by quoting the six points Barker's book makes about paradigms:

1. Paradigms strongly influence our perception of the world.
2. Because we get so good at using paradigms, we resist changing them.
3. Outsiders usually create new paradigms.
4. Practitioners must adopt new paradigms early as an act of faith because there will never be enough proof in the early stages.
5. Those who successfully shift paradigms gain new visions and approaches for solving problems.
6. A new paradigm puts everyone back to zero, so practitioners of the old paradigm, who may have had great advantages, lose much or all of that leverage. Although, I argue that the new Paradigm Shifts will drag many out beyond the breakers, never to be heard from again.

Look closely at those first two points again, particularly with regard to the three Paradigm Shift examples from Barker: the Swiss quartz watch, Xerox machines, and Japan's drive for manufacturing quality.

The Swiss did not think new technology would catch on with consumers. Within a few years, digital, quartz watches dominated the market, and the Swiss watch industry suffered,[2] although it did adapt to the new paradigm and recover.

The forty-three companies that rejected Chester Carlson's "new photography" watched Haloid Photographic Company capitalize, grow, and eventually become Xerox.

Reading that story in Barker's book, I imagine Carlson may have made a mistake by pitching electrostatic photography as photography. Investors need to have good reasons to risk their money, and back then, Carlson's idea could not have replaced photographic quality prints. Instead, Xerox took the world by storm with plain paper copying machines that were handy for business use—an idea that might have piqued more investor interest.

My favorite of the three examples, though, is Deming, whose quality management ideas align heavily with the industrial engineering curricula I studied at Purdue University. As American consumers gravitated toward Japanese products, U.S. manufacturers deployed a bevy of excuses to explain the difference—Japan had newer factories, the homogenous culture was more suited to corporate communications to produce better products, and the workforce was well-educated, among other excuses Barker cited.

Eventually, the cause—that Japan practiced better management techniques than America—could no longer be denied.

Barker does err when he says that, since then, American manufacturing has been racing to learn Deming's techniques. Much of what Deming taught consisted of basic industrial engineering principles, albeit infused with a philosophy of continuous improvement and adapted to Japanese culture.

Business actors in all three examples are akin to today's leaders who cannot wait to return to 2019, to find that sense of normalcy, to set shore on dry land, away from the turbulent surf of volatility triggered by waves of Disruptions.

That's a recipe for being permanently thrashed off your surfboard. The rules will constantly change.

Imagine hitting the beach for a lazy day surfing small waves that look about two to three feet tall. All of a sudden, the waves are cresting at more than twenty feet, what sport insiders term "big wave surfing." You head back in for your specialized gun, a board designed for such mammoths. Immediately, wave intensity diminishes, and their height drops to four or five feet. Again, you trudge onshore for a different board. Then, by the time you get back out in the surf, you and your board are trying to navigate a hurricane.

No wonder the COVID-19 era has puzzled so many business executives to the point that they want to throw up their hands, park their surfboards, and crawl under their $7,000 mahogany desks. That's a lot easier than trying to see around future corners, gain insights, develop strategies to replace obsolete paradigms, and deploy insights to stay on your surfboard, particularly when you're used to climbing the metaphorical business mountaintop and taking a well-deserved rest.

My father probably changed paradigms three times in his life. We have changed paradigms probably six times in the past year. I spent much of my life in the supply chain paradigm, adding leadership studies as I transitioned from North Carolina State University assistant professor to part-time consultant to entrepreneur to successful business leader. Even though I recognize and accept the Disruption-Tipping Point-Paradigm Shift phenomenon, I still must adjust my thinking on a constant basis.

Luckily, this era of Disruption arrived in what former IBM Global Chief Technology Officer Ben Amaba (now Vice President of Strategic Partnerships at Clarifai) calls the "Cognitive Age," an era where artificial intelligence, machine learning, cloud computing, and other advanced technologies help you pair visibility with actionability to solve your issues and then re-solve the resulting changes.

Digital Supply Networks, envisioned by me in 2003 (even

though I didn't have a name for it at the time or know how they could be done), will enable end-to-end supply chain visibility. I explain more about that Paradigm Shift in Chapter 9. Distributed Logistics, first practiced by Amazon, will help you place inventory closer to customers, cutting down service time. I detail the Distributed Logistics Paradigm Shift in Chapter 8.

Combined with embracing instead of running from Disruptions, Tipping Points, and Paradigm Shifts, you will be able to adjust and stay on your surfboard when low waves crest into big waves, back to small waves, back up to mid-sized waves, and so on, surviving and maybe even thriving.

One thing for sure is that Barker's advice rings true over thirty-five years later: "To ignore the power of paradigms to influence your judgment is to put yourself at significant risk when exploring the future."

Historically, those who understand and accept new paradigms see the world in a different way, Barker writes. He points out that scientists who view problems via new paradigms talk about seeing things they had not seen before, viewing the world as if scales have fallen from their eyes.

Two people using different paradigms to solve the same problem will come to different conclusions, and that's OK, because each problem you face will have more than one solution, particularly since you will need optionality, not optimality, to deal with the future.

While COVID-19 is the biggest Disruption of our time, humans are the ones who must notice which way the Tipping Points are headed and create new paradigms to ride the waves to success. Those who want to move forward in a world of perpetual Disruption should follow the practice of paradigm shifters who exemplified success pre-pandemic, as they are poised for post-pandemic success as well.

In my Insightful Leadership process, Paradigm shifters are the ones who successfully communicate to their team the innovations that can replace obsolete paradigms, deploy these insights, and continue surfing toward continual success.

Barker maintains that most paradigm shifters are outsiders who bring new ideas to old problems. I contend that future paradigm shifters will often need to be insiders who understand the constraints of their sectors but possess the vision to look beyond.

Tesla's Elon Musk is a nice union of the two. His initial fortune came from software companies Zip2 and PayPal. When he first invested in Tesla circa 2004, he had never been a car company executive; just like when he founded SpaceX in 2002, he had never launched a rocket into the stratosphere. He had also founded a tunneling company (The Boring Company) and neurotechnology startup (Neuralink). Both are now worth hundreds of millions of dollars.[3]

Perhaps some of these $100 million-plus companies will fail, and some won't. According to inventor, futurist, and author Ray Kurzweil, many innovations fail because the timing is wrong: "Inventing is a lot like surfing: you have to anticipate and catch the wave at just the right moment."[4]

At Tesla, Musk surrounded himself with top-notch car industry specialists. He learned and challenged what they were doing because he was trying to create an appealing electric vehicle that would be useful to drivers, not just a play toy people could drive for a couple of hours, park, and charge for the next twenty-four hours.

I don't think Musk generates all the great ideas that flow out of his companies himself. He sits around in a room full of geniuses to understand how things are done. Then, he asks questions: Why? Does that make sense? Is that a good idea? What if we did this instead?

From that comes a series of collaborative innovations, from service (technicians who make house calls or diagnose and solve problems over the internet) to distribution (no dealers with conflicts of interest stand between the car maker and the customer) to performance over time (over-the-air software updates offer continual improvements, whereas most cars' performance degrades over time).

Traditional automotive companies would never think of putting batteries underneath a car; it just wasn't an alternative. To Musk's team, it was obvious. Batteries are heavy. They should be the car's center of mass, not in the trunk or in the hood where the internal combustion engine used to be.

Musk, an outsider in the automotive industry, brought his insider knowledge of innovation from the software industry, infusing an old sector with new ideas. He brought insight—Insightful Leadership—rather than trying to convert an old piston-powered vehicle into a new breed of electric car.

This approach mitigated and avoided issues electric cars faced even though his "practices flew in the face of traditional automakers who saw insufficient testing and quality assurance."[5]

Contrary to Musk, I'm not sure Amazon's Jeff Bezos listened to a whole lot of other people. He just dreamed up the company and made it happen, more like a traditional innovator.

His previous investment banking gig might make Bezos seem like an outsider to the nascent eCommerce world, but let's take a closer look.

Bezos examined internet investment opportunities for his bank. Web usage was growing by more than 2,000% per year.[6] With computer science and electrical engineering degrees from Princeton, Bezos had the perfect position to see the wave of the future.

I believe Bezos is a supply chain guy at heart. I spoke about this in my YouTube video, "The Amazon Effect."

In fact, in October 2014, just a month after the Alibaba IPO, I gave a speech in the upstairs dining room of the 21 Club in New York City. Present were over two hundred executives from financial institutions and Wall Street. The title of my memorable speech—memorable not just for its content but for the vituperative audience reaction—was "Amazon and Alibaba: The Titans of Ecommerce."

Several were not receptive to my message that Amazon and Alibaba (the Chinese eCommerce giant co-founded by Jack Ma) would revolutionize business with what I called back then (and still call) the Amazon effect.

One audience member got up and literally screamed at me during the presentation, "You have to be an absolute idiot to think you can deliver products to someone's front door and not charge for shipping. That's absolutely stupid. I mean, do you have any intelligence at all?" He continued. "Bezos and Ma will never make a penny. Their stocks are Ponzi schemes because everybody keeps buying their BS, but those stocks are going to bomb. Are you stupid?"

Needless to say, Bezos and Ma have proven that guy 1,000% wrong, serving and delighting customers by the millions, all while growing employment numbers and investor happiness. Amazon's stock traded in the $300 range back then. Alibaba's IPO started at $68. I'll bet that everyone in that entire room wishes they had stock options at those prices.

I think Bezos saw the full picture before he sold his first online book in 1995. He understood the whole thing. He just thinks differently.

He was the first one to think of Distributed Logistics, and now, Amazon has more than one thousand distribution/fulfillment/sortation/receiving centers, stations, hubs, and stores nationwide (with another nine hundred-plus more overseas) and plans for hundreds more, positioning inventory near customers for rapid delivery.[7] All other businesses are playing catch-up.

Bezos started Amazon Web Services, changing the game for cloud computing and software as a service, beating Microsoft, Oracle, and even Google in what should have been their game.

Musk and Bezos both exemplify Barker's fourth and fifth points about paradigms: practitioners must adopt the new paradigm early as an act of faith because there never will be enough proof in its early stages, and those who successfully shift will gain new vision and new approaches for solving problems.

How many times has the business press and mass media written both off in the past twenty-five years? I'm not sure I can count that high, but for them, there was just never enough proof that Amazon and Tesla could deliver the goods.

Musk and Bezos and those who follow their lead and develop Insightful Leadership will continue to surf the waves to success. Their surfboards will not sink. Tesla's innovative car design is already spurring further innovation. Like the aerospace engineers who build wings as fuel tanks instead of building fuel tanks inside the wings, Tesla's new honeycomb-structured battery pack acts as a body structure, lining the front and rear underbody parts. The honeycomb design, as any engineer will tell you, decreases weight while adding strength. The aerospace and automotive industries use such designs for crash absorption, not to strengthen the overall body. In a world where industrial engineers often work hard for 1-2% efficiency improvements, Tesla engineers tout a 10% mass reduction, 370 fewer parts, and a 14% range increase opportunity.[8]

Fewer parts mean fewer things that break, fewer things that can go wrong, and simpler systems, all of which engineer out the possibility of failure, increasing vehicle reliability. Less weight adds to vehicle range, an area where Tesla routinely beats its competitors.

This is specifying shifts in business that provide opportunities for competitive advantage, developing strategies to replace obsolete piston-driven car designs, aligning your team to deploy those insights, and disrupting the status quo. This is Insightful Leadership that surfs the waves of Disruption to success.

This brings me to Barker's sixth point, where a new paradigm puts everyone back to zero. After all, the automotive industry is rethinking everything to compete with Tesla, and the entire world (grocery, retail, delivery services, logistics providers, Netflix, Apple, Google, etc.) is revising operations to compete with Amazon.

Many business leaders will not just lose leverage and advantages. Many will sink, washed away by Paradigm Shifts emanating from the waves of permanent Disruption.

Since March 2020, how many managers and executives have you heard wail, "When can we go back to our lives? When can we go back to normal?"

As I will make abundantly clear in this book, the answer is never. These people have their heads in the sand, not their feet on the surfboard, and their eyes certainly aren't peering around the corner for the next set of waves. New COVID-19 variants (or other diseases) will crop up. Entrepreneurs will target your sector. Innovations will abound. Inflation will rise. Disruptions will occur. Geopolitics, from shooting wars to trade wars, will raise its ugly head.

Business people and entrepreneurs used to strive to climb to the mountaintop and hoped to stay there. These days, such a rise is a fool's errand. A few insights will not lead to perpetual success in a world of perpetual Disruption. When you change your paradigm or learn a new one, Barker says the world becomes a different place. You see things differently. Previously impossible solutions become possible.

In this world, insight becomes insighting, the gerund—a continual process. For today's Insightful Leader, continual Disruptions, Tipping Points, and Paradigm Shifts will provide unlimited risk and opportunity.

Give up trying to rest on shore or on that ephemeral mountaintop. In a world where Disruption is the new normal, you must continually surf to success, wave to wave to wave to wave.

The next chapter delves deeper into the specifics of COVID-19's effects on different industries and each part of the supply chain.

1. Barker, Joel Arthur. *Discovering the Future: The Business of Paradigms.* ILI Press, 1988.
2. Louise, Emma. "The History of Quartz Watches." *First Class Watches*, 2 Feb. 2021, www.firstclasswatches.co.uk/blog/2021/02/the-history-of-quartz-watches/.
3. De la Garza, Alejandro. "How Elon Musk Built His Fortune—And Became the Richest Private Citizen in the World." *Time Magazine*, 13 Dec. 2021, time.com/6127754/elon-musk-net-worth-person-of-the-year/.
4. Kurzweil, Ray. *The Singularity Is Near: When Humans Transcend Biology.* The Penguin Group, 2005.
5. Taylor, Edward, et al. "How Tesla Defined a New Era for the Global Auto Industry." *Autoblog*, 26 July 2020, autoblog.com/2020/07/26/tesla-vs-daimler-toyota-manufacturing/.
6. "Jeff Bezos: American Entrepreneur." *Encyclopedia Brittanica*, 8 Jan. 2022, www.britannica.com/biography/Jeff-Bezos.
7. Wulfraat, Marc. "Amazon Global Supply Chain and Fulfillment Center Network." *MWPVL International Inc.*, mwpvl.com/html/amazon_com.html.
8. Lambert, Fred. "First Look at Tesla's New Structural Battery Pack That Will Power its Future Electric Cars." *Electrek*, 19 Jan. 2021, electrek.co/2021/01/19/tesla-structural-battery-pack-first-picture/.

5 THE CASCADING CHAOS OF COVID-19

In the year 2020, the Black Swan of COVID-19
mated with the concept of VUCA to spawn a brand-
new world of permanent Disruption. A catastrophic
twelve week shutdown of manufacturing in China
cascaded across the globe, with the virus always
moving faster than products and plans. Disruptions
continued in 2021. Semiconductor supply plunged
due to the pandemic, fires, and freezes. One port
exploded, and other ports were inadequate to meet
demand. Bankruptcies increased, and social upheaval
buffeted U.S. politics.

The destroyer that stopped the factory of the world was
roughly one hundred nanometers.[1]

Sizewise, the coronavirus particle that brought fear, dread,
and death to the world sounds so insignificant compared to
China's 3.7 million square miles, 1.4 billion people, and a
manufacturing sector worth nearly $4 trillion a year.

But COVID-19, a virus about 1/1000th as wide as a
human hair,[2] rained exponential death blows upon populations, manufacturing, and logistics during the early months of

2020. That's kind of like a band of zooplankton, reportedly the smallest creature in the ocean, taking down your surfboard as you try to ride the waves of Disruptions, Tipping Points, and Paradigm Shifts.

The disaster of COVID-19 was amplified by the Chinese New Year, transforming a once-a-century pandemic into a one-in-a million catastrophe. Virtually every point in the world's supply chain was hit by shutdowns, work stoppages, the virus, or all three.

Over the last two decades, China has grown into the factory of the world. In 2004, China's manufacturing output was $625.22 billion. By 2020, that figure had skyrocketed to $3.853 trillion.[3] China's share of global manufacturing output stood at 28.7% compared to 16.8% in 2019 for the United States.[4]

No, not everything is made in China, but even goods finished elsewhere often start their manufacturing process with Chinese components. It's rather difficult to find manufactured goods that don't have some input from China, such as partially or completely finished parts or raw materials.

So if China shuts down, a lot of manufacturing and supply chain activities follow.

Like France's six week vacation period every July-August, everyone in China goes home to their birthplace for the Chinese New Year. The official seven day holiday of factory closures usually stretches into two to four weeks, giving factory workers time to go home, usually to a farm or small community far away from big city factories. It takes even more time to fully ramp production back up, as Chinese workers use the off time to find better jobs or, in some cases, decide to stay home.[5] That further hampers production because, as every leader knows, training new employees to a level of experience to match the ones they replaced takes time.

The Largest Worker Migration on the Planet

It may be difficult to wrap your mind around how huge this is, as Chinese New Year is the world's largest migration. 415 million Chinese people traveled for the New Year in 2019, more than seven times the 55.3 million who traveled for Thanksgiving in 2019 in the United States. In fact, the 415 million Chinese people still dwarfed the 115.6 million Americans who traveled during Christmas and New Year's that year.[6]

Smart businesses can plan for these closures. After all, it happens every year, kind of like the Thanksgiving-Christmas rush in the United States.

While the business world has dealt with such VUCA (volatility, uncertainty, complexity and ambiguity) for years, the Black Swan of COVID-19, combined with digital innovation and growing geopolitical and financial crises, turned 2020 into VUCA on steroids.

Although January 25 was the actual calendar date of the Chinese New Year, factories always close beforehand to give their charges time to make it to their far-flung homes. So when Chinese authorities shut down Wuhan—a major manufacturing center—on January 23, it caught the world by surprise. The rest of the Hubei Province followed days later.

Wuhan's streets were deserted, apart from ambulances and security personnel, from February to March 2020. Eleven million people were confined to their homes as medical personnel from around China poured in to help Wuhan's exhausted (and often COVID-19-infected) doctors and nurses.[7]

Tens of millions of Chinese workers could not migrate back to their factories, and the brutal methods of lockdown and swift mass testing migrated from Wuhan's province to other major cities that saw significant COVID-19 spikes, including Beijing, Shanghai, and other manufacturing centers.

And while it came at a significant cost, most news agencies and medical authorities admitted that the shutdowns proved highly effective at tackling the virus.

The results for the supply chain and manufacturing world were, however, downright catastrophic.

The factories that were scheduled to reopen after the January 25, 2020 Chinese New Year stayed closed. Components and finished goods were not produced. All the orders that were supposed to ship in late January and early February were not shipped. Importers could not place new orders after the holiday, ruefully realizing that they did not have enough stock to keep up with sales.

Although the Wuhan shutdown was lifted in early April, the city was effectively sealed off from the rest of the country from January until June.[8]

After the near total months-long shutdown, workers returned. Factories reopened.

However, finished goods come from raw materials brought by truckers—truckers who had still not returned.

When the truckers finally came back (a staggered and sporadic process), the raw materials flowed again, and the factories restarted, producing automobiles and steel in Shanghai, electronics in Shenzhen, car parts, toys and apparel in Guangzhou, and mobile phone components and home decor in Dongguan.[9]

But then—you guessed it—the factories had to wait for outbound shippers to return. Finally, the outbound shippers got back on the job, delivering goods to the ports. But those goods languished in some of the busiest ports in the world—Shanghai, Shenzhen, Ningbo-Zhoushan, Guangzhou, Qingdao, and more—waiting for port operators to return to load goods onto their ships.[10]

This cavalcade of cascading catastrophes turned a six week shutdown into a twelve week virtual termination of business where none of the companies in the world received raw materials, components, finished products, or a combination of all three.

It takes herculean efforts to start recovering supply, but to get it really flowing takes twelve weeks as the whole supply world sinks in the turbulent surf. Basically, the task of producing the world's goods and supplies took a three month vacation.

And that's just the start. By then, China had added another component to its list of exports—the COVID-19 virus.

Goods travel by ship slowly. Coronavirus travels by plane quickly. Therefore, the deadliest export since the Spanish flu epidemic of 1918-1919 struck before the long-awaited products were offloaded in West Coast ports.

Closed for Commerce

Like China, Italy, and a few others in the first months of 2020, large portions of the United States shut down in March. The goal was to "flatten the curve," or reduce the growth of virus cases and take pressure off soon-to-be-overloaded health systems. Meanwhile, the shirts, pants, car parts, washing machine motors, steel for further manufacturing, and plastic toys piled up in the supply chain.

On March 31, 2020, more than one third of humanity was under some form of lockdown. Eight days later, roughly 95% of U.S. residents were under some form of lockdown from city, state, or federal authorities.[11]

Consider it the mother of all works-in-process bottlenecks.

In March, April, and May 2020, people were dying at alarming rates. Hospitals in locations hit hard by COVID-19 faced unrelenting pressure. U.S. consumers who dodged the virus worked from their homes in sweatpants and pajamas. They weren't buying new shirts—or much of anything—from traditional shopping categories. Cosmetics in particular were pummeled, suffering double digit declines.[12]

In other sectors, panic buying took hold. Hand sanitizer, cleaners, vitamin supplements, hair coloring and, yes, toilet paper flew off the shelves and from eCommerce warehouses. Demand for meat sold by grocery stores and markets skyrocketed; demand for meat sold in restaurants and hotels plunged. In fact, a working paper by the U.S. Department of Agriculture reported that "spending in restaurants and hotels fell by more than 60 percent in March, while grocery spending spiked by more than 50 percent, as people prepared more meals at home."[13]

COVID-19 spread throughout essential businesses that were allowed to remain open. This included meatpacking plants and processors. Not only did U.S. meatpackers lose workers to sickness and, even worse, death, the resulting fear increased absenteeism as workers stayed home after watching their colleagues sicken and die.

Both plant capacity and capacity utilization decreased substantially: beef production by 25%, pork production by 50%,[14] and poultry production by 15%.[15]

The meat that was produced was funneled into supply chains thrown awry by the pandemic. Restaurants, hotels, and grocery stores receive their meat from separate and specialized production processes and distribution networks. This necessitates costly supply chain transitions that contribute to higher prices and occasional stockouts at your local grocery store.[16]

Two Behind-the-Scenes Tipping Points

The behind-the-scenes stories of two products, toilet paper and porta-potties, illustrate the effects of COVID-19.

From your local news reports, you can be forgiven for thinking that COVID-19 skyrocketed the demand for toilet paper. That belief belies the fact that, just like meat and many other goods, the toilet paper market has two distinct, separate supply chains, as different from each other as socks are from shirts.

Kimberly-Clark, Georgia-Pacific, and Procter & Gamble make single-ply and two-ply. Like other large consumer packaged goods (CPG) companies, its business-to-business (B2B) supply chain sells single-ply to the Hyatt hotels, offices, and industrial sites. The business-to-consumer (B2C) supply chain services two-ply to Krogers, Safeways, Office Depots, and Walmarts. Packaging for hotels, offices, and restaurants also differs dramatically from packaging for your local mega-mart or corner store.

The toilet paper manufacturing and supply chain operations are different businesses. Prior to COVID-19, the sales and operations planning groups would have balked at the notion of intermixing these supply chains. Why would a men's store co-mingle supply chains for shoes and trousers?

The one-ply manufacturing, packaging, and supply chain processes simply won't suffice to get toilet paper into your local Target.

This is a perfect example of optimality versus my concept of optionality.

Take toilet paper, for example (and many would if they could have found rolls during the pandemic).

For decades, businesses and engineers have designed their systems to produce and deliver the right number of products as cost-efficiently as possible—optimality.

This has helped drive down the cost of goods and services, giving consumers a wide range of options at numerous price points, from the dollar stores all the way up to the Chanel, Harrods, and other shops on Rodeo Drive.

For years, the toilet paper industry "knew" how much single-ply (B2B) and two-ply (B2C) toilet paper we needed. We could design manufacturing, packaging, and supply chain systems for one or the other. Designing systems to produce and deliver both—optionality—added cost, making little sense.

When COVID-19 shut down offices and businesses, B2B

demand shut down. Conversely, demand skyrocketed on the B2C side.

And the shortage was made worse by news about the shortage. People saw empty shelves on TV and in newspapers, resulting in panic buying scenes repeated across the United States. Distressed consumers argued with checkout clerks who limited their clientele to one or two packs. Of course, customers wanted four packs because they were buying two for themselves and two for their mothers, but that didn't matter, and then they would end up in a fight with the overworked, beleaguered store staff who fretted that the customers would infect them with the dreaded virus.

The supply uncertainty came because of how Disruption can break optimal decisions.

I will discuss this more in Chapter 6, but while past Disruptions often reset history, COVID-19 accelerated it. Disruption was growing pre-COVID-19, and Disruption is never going away. Disruption is the new normal.

In the future, executives and engineers need to design their systems so they can switch on a dime. Much like how warehousing must now fulfill case orders to stores and businesses *and* each orders (single items) to eCommerce consumers, factories must be able to produce two-ply *and* one-ply. Packaging choices also need to be optional, allowing your supply chains to adjust at will to whatever Disruption is coming tomorrow or the next day.

In a world of continual Disruption, it doesn't cost too much to design and deploy optional systems. Insightful Leaders should demand that their enterprises offer optionality, the insight that leads to competitive advantage in the current and future business climate.

Somewhere, sometime, and somehow, just like toilet paper, hand sanitizer, and other product categories during COVID-19, everything you know (or think you know) about supply will be destroyed. Everything you know (or think you know) about demand will be destroyed.

Given that the goal of supply chain is to synchronize supply to demand, if you don't control supply, and if you don't have a clue about demand, then you are in the middle of the ocean without a surfboard.

In a world of uncertainty about uncertainty, you're going to need options—optionality. You don't know what you don't know, and you can't.

An optional system for making and delivering toilet paper would have allowed CPG companies to more quickly synchronize supply and demand. If the choice is nothing or one-ply, most consumers will opt for the one-ply.

Tomato juice is another prime example. Campbell's and other companies have a commercial division and a consumer division. The consumer division produces small bottles and small cans to sit on the shelves at Winn-Dixie, Kroger, and Albertsons.

The commercial division thinks industrial. If you're selling to a Marriott Hotel, your packaging mindset is around designing for large cans. In many cases—tomato juice and toilet paper are just two examples—manufacturers produce different products, different brands, and different quality for various market segments.

Yes, it's all tomato juice. But as far as the end-to-end supply chain is concerned, each product may as well be for an entirely different fruit. They're as different as Canali taupe wool dress pants and a pair of Levi's—sure, they're both pants, but that's about it.

The Porta-Potty Problem

Until February 2021, supply chain leaders paid little attention to their porta-potty portfolio.

In fact, no one realized that porta-potties had much to do with supply chain, manufacturing holdups, Insightful Leadership, or anything beyond the, well, basic necessities of human biology on construction sites, outdoor concerts, festivals and the like.

That month, the Dallas deep freeze hit, stretching all the way up to Memphis, Tennessee, where a major third party logistics provider (3PL) operates six warehouses. The nationwide operation ships everything from medical devices to apparel to consumer electronics, interacting with scores of manufacturing and logistics concerns.

When the thaw came and employees reported back to work, managers realized they didn't have water or toilets—the freeze and thaw had shattered the water mains.

The CEO told managers to go rent porta-potties. The managers replied, "There are none."

Realizing that the Midwestern U.S. porta-potty supply had disappeared, the CEO got on the horn to a manager of the 3PL's distribution center in Montebello, California.

The Montebello site manager, who we'll call Bob, scoured the entire Los Angeles-San Bernardino area, rented every porta-potty he could, put them on flatbeds, and drove three tractor-trailers of porta-potties to Memphis, a twenty-eight hour nonstop ride.

Bob's epic journey and the 3PL's porta potty problem had been repeated earlier in Texas. Beyond the deaths, discomfort, power outages, and rolling blackouts that resulted from temperatures plunging to zero degrees Fahrenheit, the severe winter storms that swept across the southern portion of the U.S. Midwest hit the Lone Star State's manufacturing sector hard.

Already reeling from chip shortages due to the coronavirus pandemic, makers of computers, automobiles, and other goods faced the shutdown of seven semiconductor plants in Texas, a center of U.S. semiconductor manufacturing.

When the thaw came, semiconductor and other manufacturing plants in Dallas faced the same problems the 3PL later dealt with in Memphis—broken water mains and no plumbing.

Companies had already gone a week without any shipments to or from their warehouses. Containers of raw materials were showing up, but they couldn't be unloaded. They had a huge amount of work to do, but they could not bring their employees back on site if they didn't have toilets.

So Texas sucked all the porta-potties out of Tennessee, Alabama, and Arkansas, too, and that's how a Memphis 3PL absconded with the porta-potty supply in California.

So for the 3PL—and many other operations in Memphis and elsewhere—it was a repeated good news/bad news pattern of getting hit in the nose, falling down, and getting back up.

The good news is the temperature went up and the power came back on. The bad news is the water main froze, and they had no water in the warehouse.

The good news is the employees returned to work. The bad news is they had to send them home because bathrooms had no water.

The good news is the plumbing situation could be alleviated by porta-potties. The bad news is that every porta-potty in the Midwest had been rented.

The good news is they found porta-potties in California. The bad news is shipping porta-potties cost $600 apiece.

The good news is the city fixed the water main. The bad news is the enterprise had to ship the porta-potties back to California at $600 each.

Think of the implications of this cascade of events. If all the porta-potties are in Memphis or Dallas, it's deuced difficult to start a construction site in California. With porta-potties in operation at manufacturing sites throughout the Midwest, construction jobs halt in that part of the United States as well. Porta-potties, like numerous other small details, can become essential to a properly functioning end-to-end supply chain.

Combining the experience of the Midwestern deep freeze with the knowledge of how important porta-potties are to manufacturing and supply chain operations, the Insightful Leader might keep a supply of porta-potties on hand or at least source a first-option contract with a local supplier. This would allow them to zoom past the competition.

In this case, riding the wave involves paying attention to the flow of, well, human excrement. Either way, adding optionality to your operations will include many different factors.

2021—A 2020 Redux and a Harbinger of the Future

After 2020, when business and supply chain leaders faced a rampaging virus, government-mandated lockdowns, sickness and death in their workforce, pallet shortages, labor shortages, a port exploding, increased social unrest, and skyrocketing bankruptcies, 2021 had to improve, right?

Not so fast, supply chain Sherlock.

Political upheaval continued when a mob of protesters invaded the U.S. Capitol building on January 6, temporarily halting congressional activities. The last time the U.S. Capitol was breached was August 24, 1814, when the British army burned large parts of the city in the War of 1812.

Protests, often violent, swept the globe from Cuba to South Africa to Colombia to Haiti, and up to thirty-seven countries might face large protest movements in the next few years. Less-developed countries also faced vaccine shortages, forcing them to live with large COVID-19 outbreaks and fueling more instability. In 2021, COVID-19 continued as an economic, social, and political crisis.[17]

Surveys, including one by the Peace Research Institute Oslo in Norway, associated mental health stresses from the pandemic with societal and government dissatisfaction. "Our investigations show that the psychological toll of living through a pandemic also stoked anti-government and anti-systemic attitudes that led to political violence in a number of countries," study author and researcher Henrikas Bartuse-vičius told *U.S. News & World Report.*[18]

Such unrest may have played a part in transitioning the lockdown Tipping Point into a working from home Paradigm Shift which, for some, became a "not-working-at-all" Paradigm Shift, as legions of employees left the workforce. News reports on the Great Resignation put the blame on extended unemployment benefits, horrible bosses, low pay, awful working conditions, stressful jobs, or a combination. As it turns out, later reports showed that baby boomers who decided to retire during COVID-19 had a lot to do with the labor shortage.[19] When millions of people retire early, those jobs have to be filled by others, and lower-wage workers have better options to move up the ladder. All of this is only a part of the unrest of 2021.

The exploded port phenomenon morphed into an over-loaded port Tipping Point, as news media reported on lines of ships waiting outside U.S. ports, particularly the notoriously inefficient ports of Long Beach and Los Angeles.

Container ships faced problems even in transit between ports. In March 2021, the *Ever Given*, one of the largest container ships in the world, got stuck in the Suez Canal, one of the most important shipping routes between East and West.

In fact, that 120 mile long waterway handles about 12% of global trade, 30% of global container traffic, and more than $1 trillion worth of goods a year.[20]

And the semiconductor shortage, exacerbated in February 2021 with the aforementioned Dallas deep freeze, was only worsened by a fire at Renesas in Japan, which produced 17% of the planet's automotive semiconductor chips.[21] Makers of cars, computers, electronics, and medical devices saw their supplies of needed semiconductors curtailed or completely cut off even as demand for consumer goods skyrocketed, a Black Swan for those businesses indeed.

Semiconductor supplies could be limited for quite some time. The world's largest contract manufacturer of chips, Taiwan Semiconductor Manufacturing Company, had to truck water into its plants to maintain production after severe drought restricted the company's use of tap water.[22]

In the late summer of 2021, more than a year after the initial shutdowns, major news media outlets—not just supply chain publications—were warning of increased temporary stockouts of many goods, along with a nod to preparing for the fact that, due to supply chain concerns, future holiday shopping seasons need to begin... in September.

Since COVID-19 burst onto the scene, you've faced trucker, worker, pallet, equipment, and semiconductor shortages; cost and capacity constraints; shipping disasters; and bottlenecks all up and down your supply chain. In 2020 and 2021, supply chain was in a fight, got punched in the nose and knocked down, then got back up again only to get punched in the nose and knocked down again.

At some point, you ask yourself, "Do I really want to get up again? This is not fun, and my face hurts."

Well, yes, you must get up again. Not only that, but you must understand that 2020 and 2021 are not aberrations on the way back to a time of normalcy.

Disruption is the new normal. The Insightful Leader understands this and can use this knowledge to ride the waves of Disruptions-Tipping Points-Paradigm Shifts into a successful future.

---

1. Lee, Byung Uk. "Minimum Sizes of Respiratory Particles Carrying SARS-CoV-2 and the Possibility of Aerosol Generation." *International Journal of Environmental Research and Public Health*, vol. 17, no. 19, 23 Sep. 2020, pp. 1-8. *PubMed*, doi:10.3390/ijerph17196960.

2. Ang, Carmen. "This Is How Coronavirus Compares to the World's Smallest Particles." *World Economic Forum*, 15 Oct. 2020, weforum.org/agenda/2020/10/covid-19-coronavirus-disease-size-compairson-zika-health-air-pollution.

3. "China Manufacturing Output 1960-2021." *Macrotrends*, macrotrends.net/countries/CHN/china/manufacturing-output.

4. Richter, Felix. "China Is the World's Manufacturing Superpower." *Statista*, 4 May 2021, statista.com/chart/20858/top-10-countries-by-share-of-global-manufacturing-output/.

5. "Chinese New Year Shutdown 2022: Avoid Problems With Your Factory." *Insight Quality Services*, 16 Sept. 2021, insight-quality.com/chinese-new-year-factory-shutdown/.

6. McCarthy, Niall. "The World's Largest Human Migration Is About To Begin." *Statista*, 22 Jan. 2020, statista.com/chart/12916/the-worlds-largest-migration-is-about-to-begin/.

7. "Timeline: China's COVID-19 outbreak and lockdown of Wuhan." *The Associated Press*, 22 Jan. 2021, apnews.com/article/pandemics-wuhan-china-coronavirus-pandemic-e6147ecoff88affb99c811149424239d.

8. Illmer, Andreas, et al. "Wuhan Lockdown: A Year of China's Fight Against the Covid Pandemic." *BBC*, 22 Jan. 2021, bbc.com/news/world-asia-china-55628488.

9. Shaw, Sharline. "Best 20 China Manufacturing Cities." *Leeline Sourcing*, 8 Feb. 2022, leelinesourcing.com/china-manufacturing-cities/.

10. Donnelly, Jack. "What are the Five Top Ports in China?" *Port Technology*, 18 Feb. 2020, porttechnology.org/news/what-are-the-top-ports-in-china/.

11. Neilson, Susie, and Aylin Woodward. "A Comprehensive Timeline of the Coronavirus Pandemic at 1 year, from China's First Case To the Present." *Business Insider*, 24 Dec. 2020, businessinsider.com/coronavirus-pandemic-timeline-history-major-events-2020-3.

12. "How COVID–19 Has Transformed Consumer Spending Habits." *J.P.-Morgan*, 23 Nov. 2020, jpmorgan.com/solutions/cib/research/covid-spending-habits.

13. Balagtas, Joseph, and Joseph Cooper. "The Impact of Coronavirus COVID-19 on U.S. Meat and Livestock Markets." *U.S. Department of Agriculture*, Mar. 2021, usda.gov/sites/default/files/documents/covid-impact-livestock-markets.pdf.

14. Reiley, Laura. "Meat Processing Plants are Closing Due to Covid-19 Outbreaks. Beef Shortfalls May Follow." *The Washington Post*, 16 Apr. 2020, washingtonpost.com/business/2020/04/16/meat-processing-plants-are-closing-due-covid-19-outbreaks-beef-shortfalls-may-follow/.

15. McDougal, Tony. "Poultry Plants in the US Affected by Covid-19." *Poultry World*, 8 May 2020, poultryworld.net/Meat/Articles/2020/5/Poultry-plants-in-the-US-affected-by-Covid-19-580294E/.

16. Balagtas, Joseph, and Joseph Cooper. "The Impact of Coronavirus COVID-19 on U.S. Meat and Livestock Markets." *U.S. Department of Agriculture*, Mar. 2021, usda.gov/sites/default/files/documents/covid-impact-livestock-markets.pdf.

17. Labott, Elise. "Get Ready for a Spike in Global Unrest." *Foreign Policy*, 22 July 2021, foreignpolicy.com/2021/07/22/covid-global-unrest-political-upheaval/.

18. Preidt, Robert. "Pandemic Stresses Enough to Trigger Political, Social Unrest: Analysis." *U.S. News & World Report*, 11 Aug. 2021, usnews.com/news/health-news/articles/2021-08-11/pandemic-stresses-enough-to-trigger-political-social-unrest-analysis.

19. Shortal, Jana. "'The Great Retirement': Majority of Employees Leaving Workforce During COVID-era." *KARE11*, 23 Feb. 2022, kare11.com/article/news/local/breaking-the-news/the-great-retirement-majority-of-

employees-leaving-workforce-during-covid-era/89-96252310-2d55-4105-b998-f691d4985f82.

20. "The Importance of the Suez Canal to Global Trade." *New Zealand Foreign Affairs and Trade*, 18 Apr. 2021, mfat.govt.nz/kr/trade/mfat-market-reports/market-reports-mi.

21. Obe, Mitsuru. "Renesas CEO Warns of Tight Chip Supply Through Mid-2022." *Nikkei Asia*, 29 July 2021, asia.nikkei.com/Business/Tech/Semiconductors/Renesas-CEO-warns-of-tight-chip-supply-through-mid-2022.

22. Cheung, Eric. "The Chipmaking Factory of the World is Battling Covid and the Climate Crisis." *CNN*, 10 June 2021, cnn.com/2021/06/10/tech/taiwan-chip-shortage-covid-climate-crisis-intl-hnk/index.html.

6 THE MOTHER OF ALL DISRUPTIONS ACCELERATED HISTORY

Unlike previous Disruptions of the last century, COVID-19 didn't freeze, slow, or reverse history; it accelerated it.

The Great Depression froze history. In many ways, 1939 was a return to 1929.

The Great Recession of 2008-2009 reversed history, resulting in greater financial regulations.

On the other hand, COVID-19 created not one, not two, but *three* Tipping Points (lockdowns, the growth of eCommerce, and broken supply chains) accelerating trends already present in daily life. We will never go back to the conditions of 2019. Previously, great leaders articulated visions of the future and aligned their operations to achieve those visions, avoiding Disruptions, or waves. You can't avoid the waves now. Insightful Leaders will ride those waves to accelerate profitable growth and success.

In Washington Irving's classic short story, Rip Van Winkle took a twenty-year nap and missed the American Revolution. His lesser-known descendant, Rip Van Supply Chain, has a somewhat different tale to tell.

When Rip Van Supply Chain went to sleep in early 2020, his systems had it made.

The enterprise had added AI-powered robotic material handling to many of its fulfillment centers. Enterprise software linked with other supply chain and manufacturing partners, giving managers good visibility into potential problems long before their competitors.

By April 2020, when he woke up from his nap, everything was chaos—and his enterprise was a good ten years behind where it needed to be. In the COVID-19 and post-COVID-19 eras of perpetual Disruptions-Tipping Points-Paradigm Shifts, with hard work and perseverance, Rip Van Supply Chain and every other organization would be lucky to almost catch up, only to fall behind again as newer Disruptions create more Tipping Points that cause new Paradigm Shifts.

Insightful Leadership, the kind that peers around the corners well outside of your sector's sphere to understand trends, political changes, the legal landscape, and technology changes, is the only way your enterprise can surf the waves of Paradigm Shifts in the midst of the mother of the mother of the mother of all Disruptions.

The Disruption of COVID-19 created the waves that spawned three gargantuan Tipping Points that accelerated history:

1. COVID-19 lockdowns sent legions of people home to work.
2. Digital innovation allowed for the explosion of eCommerce demand.
3. Work from home, eCommerce, and geopolitical and financial crises combined to cause the failure of traditional supply chain management.

Happening simultaneously, those Tipping Points have created Paradigm Shifts in all facets of life: how people work, live, shop, exercise, and learn, all necessitating Paradigm Shifts in how we produce goods and services and deliver them in our supply chains, now and in the future.

Really? The Mother of the Mother of the Mother...?

When looking through centuries of human history, can I really call COVID-19 the mother of the mother of the mother of all Disruptions? Since the dawn of the 20th century, Earth's population has experienced World War I and World War II, the war between Russia and Ukraine (what some are calling World War 2.5), the advent of the personal computer, the dissolution of the Soviet Union and end of the Cold War, the rise of the internet, the September 11 terrorist attacks, and, of course, the Great Depression.

The Great Depression certainly lasted longer, beginning with the stock market crash of October 1929 and ending in 1939 or after World War II, depending on which history book you read.

That dark era produced alarming statistics. At their lowest points, U.S. industrial production plunged 47% and real gross domestic product (GDP) by 30%. Deflation took hold as the wholesale price index dropped 33%. Unemployment topped 20%.[1]

In 1932, 273,000 people lost their homes. In 1933, lenders foreclosed on one thousand mortgages a day. That same year saw 200,000 farms face foreclosure. Overall, one third of U.S. farmers lost their property between 1929 and 1933.[2]

Starving families would eat chicken soup—if they could find three-day-old chickens. Entire families lived under railroad tracks, in shantytowns, or in makeshift encampments derisively dubbed "Hoovervilles" after U.S. President Herbert Hoover.[3]

The only people doing well? Gangsters who became famous by adopting personas as "Robin Hoods," stealing from banks and giving to the poor. Some infamous gangsters include Pretty Boy Floyd, Al Capone, and the Bonnie and Clyde duo.

The economic devastation from that dark era clearly dwarfs the COVID-19 woes of the world in 2020 and 2021, especially in richer countries that provided trillions of dollars in economic stimulus.

Instead of accelerating history, though, the Great Depression froze it. If you take 1939 as the Great Depression's final year, the Roaring Twenties simply stopped and then returned. If Rip Van Supply Chain lay down for a nap in 1929 and woke up in 1939, he would look around and think his sleep lasted one evening, not ten years.

In fact, the change in the United States's GNP from 1929 to 1939 was zero. From 1919 to 1929, the average rate of U.S. unemployment was 4%, then 5% from 1939 to 1949.[4]

World War I and World War II slaughtered millions of people and changed national boundary lines, particularly in Europe and the Middle East. The Soviet Union's dissolution increased access to markets formerly behind the Iron Curtain. However, business remained fundamentally the same throughout those decades, and wars among multinational alliances have been going on for centuries.

The advent of the personal computer and the rise of the internet certainly played a part in the evolution of supply chain as a profession (and certainly will allow you to deploy Distributed Logistics and Digital Supply Networks as solutions). However, by definition, evolution is slow, incremental change over time, not a reversal.

Stock markets plunged after the September 11, 2001 terrorist attacks on the World Trade Center and the Pentagon, and U.S. foreign policy has largely been centered on wars and conflict since then. But again, outside of military personnel, their families, and anyone involved in security procedures, how we lived, worked, shopped, learned, and went about our daily lives remained similar.

After decades of what many tout as deregulation, the Great Recession of 2008-2009 reversed that, resulting in greater financial regulations, including the Dodd-Frank Act and the Emergency Economic Stabilization Act.

So how do I justify calling COVID-19 the mother of the mother of the mother of all Disruptions?

Two words: supply chain.

Back in the 1920s and 1930s, most supply chains were short and domestic. You bought goods from the general store down the street or the shop on the corner. You made things and sold them in local markets or to the guy up the street. They were short value chains indeed, and the implications of shutting down the supply chain were less important. In fact, nobody even thought in terms of supply chain, a phrase that didn't come into use until decades later.

In 1929, U.S. total foreign trade (the value of exports and imports) totaled only $7.3 billion, its largest value in years.[5] Various inflation calculators peg that as $109.1 billion in 2019 dollars.

However, by 2019, the United States was the second largest exporter and number one importer of goods with foreign trade valued at $4.1 trillion ($1.6 trillion in exports and $2.5 trillion in imports). The U.S. was also the world's largest exporter and importer of services, with $875.8 billion in service exports and $588.4 billion in service imports.[6]

This means that modern U.S. foreign trade in services alone, not even including goods, dwarfs total U.S. foreign trade before and during the Great Depression.

Foreign trade, by definition, means supply chains that stretch beyond borders. The complexity and length of today's global supply chains far exceed the complexity and length of the 1929 supply chains. Back then, supply chains didn't have to worry about surfing across the seven seas.

But by 2020, supply chains had morphed into gargantuan, complex entities. Most supply chains, and there are many, start out in Asia regardless of where the products eventually end up. Raw materials, partially finished goods, and completely manufactured products will literally go through hundreds of hands if you include all the different handoffs.

Someone harvests raw material. A trucker takes that raw material to a factory. That factory combines it with numerous raw materials from other sources. That factory manufactures parts, which get trucked to a port. Stevedores load the parts onto a ship, which crosses the ocean. More stevedores unload the parts. Truckers take them to another plant where they combine with parts from another supply chain to complete the product. The completed product gets trucked to a warehouse. Perhaps the product heads to a retail store, or less-than-truckloads forward deploy small amounts of inventory closer to populations, and warehouse personnel break down the cases and ship "eaches" (one item at a time) to eCommerce customers (the genesis of Distributed Logistics).

There are lots of opportunities for Disruption just by the natural number of things happening at any given moment. In April 2020, just a few months after COVID-19 exploded into the world's consciousness, everybody became aware of supply chains; many news industry veterans remarked that they reported about supply chains more often in 2020 than in all of their previous decades combined.

COVID-19 had longer-lasting, farther-reaching impacts because the total shutdown of supply chains was a harbinger of the new era of perpetual Disruption.

In the end, despite the harrowing years of 2020 and 2021, a devastating virus, and the millions of unfortunate deaths, COVID-19 will be remembered less by historians because of the virus and more because it was the event that changed the world.

Beyond the health and economic devastations that are largely beyond their control, business leaders and entrepreneurs should be looking at what we've learned, gaining insights, harnessing those insights to determine which Disruptions will lead to Tipping Points that will evolve into Paradigm Shifts, and deploy innovations to ride those Disruptions into future success.

Because, in relation to the acceleration of history, the pandemic is clearly the Disruption of our time.

COVID-19 has changed the way we live.

COVID-19 has changed the way we work.

COVID-19 has changed the way we shop.

COVID-19 has changed the way we raise our families.

COVID-19 has changed the way we learn.

COVID-19 has changed the way we find entertainment.

COVID-19 has changed the way we do everything.

And COVID-19 has changed the way businesses, entrepreneurs, and supply chains deliver our goods and services. The remote work explosion, combined with the massive shift to eCommerce, broke supply chains—all equally big, all interacting with one another, all happening simultaneously.

We've always had uncertainty. Now we have uncertainty about uncertainty. In the world of perpetual Disruption, the speed and magnitude of Disruptions will accelerate the problems executives and entrepreneurs must handle. This is part of what I mean when I say COVID-19 accelerated history.

Old-style leadership looks at problems in a negative fashion: they are issues to be handled. Alternatively, Insightful Leaders take the positive view—if we ride the wave of these Disruptions, Tipping Points, and Paradigm Shifts, we can surf right past our competitors.

Today, most organizations are equipped to deal with either magnitude or speed, not both. They have no idea exactly when or where these Disruptions will hit, but they can anticipate and prepare.

If a hurricane or storm spawns a tornado that strikes Charlotte, North Carolina, it's a huge disaster. But for a multi-site enterprise, particularly a global conglomerate, that's a disaster for its Charlotte operations.

Companies have built-in resilience to handle such exigencies—the Disruptions they can predict and anticipate. These disasters have limited impacts. Companies have other resources they can redeploy.

If the Charlotte warehouse is down, they can shift that capacity to Atlanta. If a trucking company goes on strike, they can ramp up deliveries through a third-party logistics partner. If a unionization effort shuts down a port, they route deliveries elsewhere.

And if it's a change that continues over years, operations can adapt and revise.

But when you have something that's both quick and of huge magnitude, whole new paradigms are going to be created, and the Disruption is going to be monumental.

Well, the mother of the mother of the mother of all Disruptions was COVID-19. While the pandemic woke up the supply chain world, the fact of the matter is that continual Disruptions from 2020 through 2022 that had nothing to do with COVID-19—the Ever Given getting stuck in the Suez Canal, a parade of business bankruptcies, the Dallas deep freeze that closed seven microchip plants, hurricanes, wildfires, social upheaval in the wake of the murder of George Floyd, the Beirut port explosion, war in Ukraine, the potential scourge of inflation, and more—will remain with us, being repeated in whole or in part in other sectors of the world, partly because the world is changing and partly because COVID-19 accelerated history.

Unless you're part of a merry band of pranksters or, say, Batman's nemesis the Joker, human nature considers Disruption problematic. Now that Disruption is the new normal, such thinking must change.

More Joker than Batman, you must welcome Disruption as an opportunity to improve, not a problem to manage.

Disruption is a chance for Insightful Leaders to anticipate where the market will move, not an attack for old-style leaders to hunker down and fight.

Disruption will lead to Tipping Points that will shift paradigms, creating entirely new markets, accelerating others, and destroying more.

Disruptions are simply indicators of where we are going, whether you like it or not.

Disruptions are coming. You can't avoid the waves. They are a natural part of today's business and life, and Insightful Leaders must embrace them, learn from them, and figure out how to get better by using Disruptions as indicators of which Tipping Point is going to create the next Paradigm Shift.

The Insightful Leader who can watch a Disruption at its early stages and anticipate where it's going rather than try to manage it away will be able to define new strategies to replace obsolete paradigms, bring their entire organization or team onto the wave of change, deploy those insights, and ride the wave of Disruptions-Tipping Points-Paradigm Shifts to entrepreneurial success and profitable growth.

You cannot stop the waves. You can only hope to ride them.

---

1. Romer, Christina D. "Great Depression." *Encyclopedia Britannia*, 2021, updated 11 Oct. 2021, https://www.britannica.com/event/Great-Depression.

2. "Housing 1929-1941." *Encyclopedia.com*, www.encyclopedia.com/education/news-and-education-magazines/housing-1929-1941. Accessed 5 Nov. 2021.

3. Gregory, James. "The Great Depression in Washington State: Hoovervilles and Homelessness." *The University of Washington, The Great Depression in Washington State Project*, 2009, depts.washington.edu/depress/hooverville.shtml.

4. "Statistics: The Impact of the Great Depression." *Gilder Lehrman Institute of American History*, www.gilderlehrman.org/history-resources/teaching-resource/statistics-impact-depression. Accessed 5 Nov. 2021

5. Boeckel, Richard M. "Foreign Trade of the United States." *Editorial Research Reports 1930*, vol. IV, CQ Press, 1930, pp. 735-52. CQ Researcher, 6 June 2022, library.cqpress.com/cqresearcher/cqresrre1930110100.

6. "Countries & Regions." *United States Trade Representative*, ustr.gov/countries-regions.

7 A TRIUMVIRATE OF TIPPING POINTS

The three Tipping Points of the last few years—lockdowns, eCommerce, and broken supply chains—have combined to alter all aspects of life. At the peak of COVID-19 in May 2020, 61% of the U.S. employee base worked from home, up from 17% before COVID-19. Even eighty-year-old grandmothers who loved spending time shopping at stores learned to shop online (and sometimes even enjoy it). Supply chains, which had traditionally balanced supply to demand, now experienced both huge inventory overages and shortages. New internet sites were created to inform people when stores received shipments of toilet paper. Global chaos reigned.

Black Friday in September? How about July? You've got to be kidding me.

But thanks to the waves of three great Tipping Points—the lockdowns, the eCommerce explosion, and broken supply chains—that's exactly what happened in 2021. And with supply chain issues ranging from consumer goods to semiconductors, Black Fridays in September could be a permanent Paradigm Shift—until the next Disruption, that is.

What created these Tipping Points? It seems rather straightforward; lockdowns more than doubled the percentage of people who worked from home. Travel restrictions left people unable to spend money on experiences. Taxpayer-funded stimulus checks left people with more money. Fear kept many people from waltzing around suddenly short-staffed stores. Digital innovation allowed eCommerce to move from a realm of "delivery-only" to "delivery-or-buy-online-and-pick-up-in-store."

All of the above factors concurrently tipped, going from small ocean waves to tsunamis in a span of weeks and striking society and business like a three-wave hold-down swamping a struggling surfer.

While surfing is largely safe, particularly when compared to BASE jumping, wingsuit flying, or Himalayan mountain-climbing, the niche of big wave surfing carries a bit more risk.

Special boards are necessary to handle towering waves that can smack and pin surfers to the ocean floor, causing head, spinal, trunk, and pelvic injuries; pneumothoraces; punctured eardrums; torn ligaments; fractured bones; and disorientation of the formerly high-flying victims.[1] Once back on the surface, there will always be the risk that a second and even a third big wave will push the surfers down. Three-wave hold-downs are survivable, but they're hardly pleasant.[2]

That three-wave smackdown that struck the world in 2020 has yet to let up. And while our aforementioned surfer can pop up from such big waves to find the ocean pretty much the same (after they recover from bruises and maybe broken bones), society and businesses do not have that luxury.

Far from receding back into the ocean depths (or the bat and pangolin populations), the waves of Disruption became Tipping Points that changed our world forever.

Why did these three Tipping Points have enough staying power to create Paradigm Shifts, whereas so many others drift into history? Think about it—when was the last time you petted your rock or guzzled a Pepsi Clear?

Let's call these reasons the three S's—speed, scope, and synchronicity. All three of the Tipping Points happened quickly, all three affected huge parts of everyone's business and personal lives, and all three happened at virtually the same time.

Tipping Point No. 1, lockdowns: Within a few months after coronavirus entered the world's consciousness via mass media, politicians had locked down much of society, moves that involved every aspect of life in numerous countries spanning every continent.

Tipping Point No. 2, eCommerce: With stores closed, consumers turned to eCommerce in unprecedented waves. Even eighty-year-old grandmothers who had never bought anything online before moved much of their shopping to the virtual world, some learning to surf the web for the first time. Demand skyrocketed as purchases of everything—especially such bare necessities as toilet paper—deluged eCommerce vendors. Sometimes fueled by government stimulus payments, consumers who couldn't spend their disposable income on travel, experiences, and dining out bought more stuff, adding pressure to groaning global supply chains.

Tipping Point No. 3, broken supply chains: At some point within the twelve week period detailed in Chapter 5, supply chains shut down along practically every link worldwide. Even essential manufacturing and logistics links that never closed or didn't shut down for long suffered from waves of sickness and death, limiting goods on the supply side. On the demand side, store shutdowns and government restrictions curtailed overall retail sales in early 2020, but eCommerce exploded and remained at levels supply chain leaders (even me!) did not expect for another five to ten years.

Although more people want to shop online, the logistics resources that deliver goods are physical entities—think trucks, ships, planes, trains, ports, automobiles, and distribution centers—operated by a combination of automation and human personnel. None of those can scale up as quickly and easily as the decision by millions of consumers to click the "Add to Cart" button.

And the waves of all three Tipping Points crashed together simultaneously, synchronicity at its best—or its worst if you're an entrepreneur, business leader, or supply chain professional trying to keep up with ever-shifting demand.

Insightful Leaders, due to their knowledge of Tipping Points and current industry paradigms, are able to anticipate that Tipping Points will shift paradigms, thus having insight as to which innovations are needed to harness the power of Paradigm Shifts. Their insights lead them to solutions and strategies that replace obsolete paradigms, keeping their enterprises surfing ahead of the competition.

How Lockdown Became a Tipping Point

Remote work has been a futuristic concept for quite some time. The manufacturing press has discussed "dark factories," where everything is fully automated so there is no need for the lights to be on, since at least the 1980s.

Despite a few working examples in Japan and the Netherlands (and even those can only run "dark" for a period of time or they still require humans for quality assurance or routine maintenance), lights-out manufacturing still remains a futuristic concept.[3]

But the 20th century Disruptions of the internet and the

rise of the personal computer made it easier for the white-collar set to operate at home. Before COVID-19 struck, about 17% of the U.S. workforce worked remotely five or more days a week,[4] a sharp and steady rise from the 6.6% in 2010.[5] As for the other 83% of the U.S. workforce, factory workers still commuted to factories; barbers, hair stylists, and tattoo artists still commuted to their shops; warehouse workers still loaded trucks; grocery store employees still unloaded trucks and stocked shelves; and cashiers still checked customers out at the end of their shopping sojourns.

So when the coronavirus ripped through society in early 2020, white-collar employees had it made. High-speed internet let executives, marketers, coders, accountants, software engineers, IT specialists, artificial intelligence personnel, and more commute from their beds to their computers.

Fear of the virus kept many people from going to the store, so they ordered goods online. Retailers, from grocery chains to department stores, started offering more options for consumers to buy online and pick up their orders in the store, even offering curbside takeout.

During the coronavirus outbreak, 58% percent of workers with at least a bachelor's degree worked remotely full-time.[6] Overall, a staggering 61% of U.S. employees worked from home at the height of the pandemic.[7]

Even more impressive has been remote work's staying power. After the pandemic, experts have predicted that somewhere between 20% of all labor[8] will work exclusively away from the office, with that number skyrocketing to 70% if work from home is defined as remotely working at least five days a month.[9] (If more Insightful Leaders embrace the future, at least 40% of the U.S. workforce could do away with commuting to the office.[10])

As time went on and society partially returned to in-person operations, more people found that they liked working from home. They enjoyed the flexibility of getting to know their children, personally feeding them breakfast instead of racing out the door for a nightmare commute, and taking a break to walk the dog for a few minutes after lunch. When schools and other activities reopened, they could walk their children to the bus stop and even go watch their recital or school play—all important life activities that many missed out on.

As a result, more than half of those workers say they would prefer to work from home after the pandemic ends, and the majority of white-collar workers can do their jobs from home.[11]

Working from home, people relied on technology, skyrocketing eCommerce orders and purchases of consumer goods. Their entire sociology of life—how they worked, shopped, and interacted with the world—changed.

If this had been a temporary blip, a few weeks to lower the curve, tamp down the COVID-19 surge, and get everything back to normal, perhaps the lockdown Tipping Point would not have spawned the Paradigm Shift of an entirely changed sociology of life. In March 2020, business gatherings, conferences, events, travels, and vacations scheduled for April and May 2020 remained on the books often until the last minute before being canceled, postponed, or turned virtual.

Not many people were peering around the corners expecting that, two years into the pandemic, work from home would be here to stay, whether the bosses like it or not.

In the midst of all the chaos, businesses started complaining that they could not find enough workers to fill desperately needed jobs. Depending on their political persuasions, people blamed what was dubbed the Great Resignation on different factors. Government stimulus money made it possible for workers to stay home and not get paid, poor pay and bad bosses made workers less than eager to return, employees took stock of their work-life balance and decided the life part was lacking, or a combination of those reasons and more made people ultimately decide to quit their jobs.

While all those likely played some part, two different culprits emerged: early retirement and entrepreneurship.

As of January 2022, nearly 70% of the five million people who left the labor force during the pandemic were older than 55. Many of them aren't looking to return. Others who seek to return compete with younger workers and often lose out.[12]

My sister-in-law, a college professor, is a prime example. College administrators limited the size of online classes, so she had to teach twice as many classes and twice as many labs for the same pay. Technological solutions—taping lectures and having multiple classes view the recordings, Zooming more than twenty-five students in class at a time—didn't seem to be options. Exhausted, she retired.

The "supply chain" for teaching biology requires facilities, books, and biology teachers. Now, that college has to find another biology professor to "fix" that supply chain.

In that respect, COVID-19 is the thief that keeps on taking.

A friend of mine in a grocery store cooperative is another example. Given the chance to work from home, this family man realized how much family activity he had missed while driving his daily commute. He discovered a whole new rhythm of life.

As his cooperative started bringing staff back to the office, my friend had second thoughts. Because of the health issue, coworkers were skittish about gathering in small conference rooms, so they still conducted most meetings via Zoom. They were literally ten feet apart in separate rooms on the same Zoom call as opposed to sitting around a table wearing masks.

He thought, "Why am I driving an hour to get to a building to resume discussions on a video chat?" But management didn't see it that way, wanting people back in the office.

My friend preferred at least a hybrid approach if not total work from home. Negotiating his new contract proved thornier than past discussions. It became increasingly difficult to define how many days he should work at home versus how many days he should commute to the office. He took a job at another grocery chain that offered more flexible arrangements. His old company was left searching for a senior VP level position.

Work from home comprises three groups: those who always want to work in the office, those who never want to go into the office, and those who prefer the hybrid approach. The hybrid approach is the dominant preference among employees, ranging from 50%[13] to 67%.[14]

But what does hybrid mean as the lockdown Tipping Point has swept the old expectations away into a new paradigm? Employers might say it's working from home one day a week while employees might only want to commute to the office one day a month. Those are entirely different mindsets that are bound to conflict, so the "I quit and go somewhere else" movement is quite real.

Others are saying, "I quit and start something else," as entrepreneurship is also on the rise.

Millennials have grown up watching Steve Jobs, Bill Gates, Elon Musk, and others create entirely new industries. To many of them, the idea of getting a job like their mother or father and working 40 hours a week for General Electric or General Motors is the beginning of dying, while the idea of entrepreneurship is the beginning of birth.

My wife and I funded a Certificate in Entrepreneurship program at my alma mater, Purdue University. Current Purdue President Mitch Daniels has taken that program from a three to a ten on a scale of one to ten. He recently told me that thousands of students now attend Purdue because it has a great entrepreneurship program.

The millennial entrepreneurial mindset and the COVID-19 pandemic have led many more people to try and surf toward their future and take charge of their lives by starting their own businesses.

An average of 452,000 new business applications were filed each month in 2021, a sharp increase from the 293,000 monthly new business applications in 2019, the year before the pandemic.[15] Other predictors expect seventeen million new U.S. businesses to get off the ground in 2022.[16]

These people are doing their own environmental scanning for their futures—peering around corners, if you will—and not liking what they see from corporate America.

So the employees you're looking for in the so-called Great Resignation might be retired, might be starting their own businesses, or might have moved on to greener pastures, taking the spots vacated by retirees or budding entrepreneurs. Good luck getting the $1.29 double cheeseburger in the future.

Because of the lockdowns, the work from home Paradigm Shift is here to stay.

How eCommerce Became a Tipping Point

The lockdown Tipping Point that begat the work-from-home Paradigm Shift led to problems elsewhere, as lockdowns had a disparate impact on lower- and middle-income workers. Most of them said they could not do their jobs from home.[17] Essential industries had difficulty functioning in isolation or with social distancing measures. Therefore, essential workers came to the office, the warehouse, the food processors, the grocery store, healthcare centers, and more, suffering massive Disruption from COVID-19 sickness and death.

The work-from-home set, on the other hand, had more disposable income from government stimulus payments, and no vacations, travel, or entertainment options to spend that cash on. The specter of COVID-19 made many fear the store. Sure, they needed bacon and toilet paper, but death stalked the aisles of the local Safeway.

So millions turned to Instacart, DoorDash, Uber Eats, buy-online-pick-up-in-store services, and other eCommerce options.

All of that disposable income piled into eCommerce just as supply was drying up, creating another Tipping Point.

For years, commentators have speculated about how eCommerce would dominate in the future. The digital innovation necessary for such a shift has been around. Now, that shift is here and accelerating.

According to the Census Bureau, U.S. retail sales increased an astonishing 31.8% from the first quarter of 2020 to the second quarter, a total of $211.5 billion. Quarter two 2020 eCommerce sales were 44.5% higher than quarter two in 2019. On the other hand, overall retail sales declined 3.9% from quarter one of 2020 to quarter two and 3.4% from the previous year.

That means that eCommerce, which has steadily grown since the dawn of the 21st century, grew from 10.1% of overall retail sales to 16.1%, a staggering increase in such a short time.

That eighty-year-old grandmother who would never deign to order online? The one who still loves the feel of a retail store and shopping? Well, with COVID-19 proving much deadlier for older people than youths, she tentatively branched out into online shopping, liked it, and is continuing to click and shop. The Target, Kroger, and Walmart parking lots filled with numbered spaces where customers would park and wait for curbside delivery. Many grocery stores debuted lockers where staff would store refrigerated online orders until pickup.

Since its initial flurry in early 2020, eCommerce has dropped some, but as of the first quarter of 2022, it totaled 14.3% of all retail sales, a significant increase.[18]

Along the way, our expectations about shopping have changed and been shaped by the response of retailers. Before the Disruptions of the last few years, if you wanted to go shopping, you went to the store. You wanted to feel the fabric. You wanted to try the suit on to make sure the shoulders fit.

Shopping was the process of selecting and deciding in person. Buying, on the other hand, was picking up a jar of peanut butter. It really didn't matter which jar of Skippy or Peter Pan.

Amazon, as usual, is disrupting even that idea. The online behemoth partnered with Kohl's in 2019, when the department store started accepting Amazon returns.

My wife Shari recently took five Amazon items to Kohl's as returns. She didn't have to package them up, affix return labels, and drive to the post office, UPS, or FedEx. Once in the store, bam—five minutes later, the returns were complete.

Before this partnership, Shari and many others would not have bought apparel online. They wanted to shop—try it on, make sure that shade of red was the right one. Online returns, from her viewpoint, were a hassle.

Many others who also looked askance at buying clothes online would follow. Amazon partnered with brick-and-mortar retail to increase apparel volume, causing further Disruption.

Amazon's environmental scan recognized the fact that many were loath to buy apparel online. An easy return policy via a brick-and-mortar store helped alleviate that concern. Its strategy shift to create a new paradigm involved partnering with another organization.

In other words, Amazon reacted to Disruption by causing more Disruption.

The benefit to Kohl's? While there, Shari saw two nice sweaters at good prices and brought them home. For Kohl's and other brick-and-mortar stores, foot traffic is the first thing they need to survive. In fact, in 2020, year one of the pandemic, Kohl's reported that its Amazon partnership drew more than two million new customers into its stores.[19]

Truly, eCommerce is 1) here to stay, 2) continuing to grow, and 3) going to be the source of more Disruptions in an age where Disruption is the new normal.

How Broken Supply Chains Became a Tipping Point

Much of that eCommerce Tipping Point, of course, comes from Asia. China in particular is known for its exports, but other Asian countries from Taiwan to Japan to Vietnam and others export cars, semiconductors, apparel, electrical machinery, leather goods, steel, food, and more to the United States, totaling hundreds of billions of dollars a year.

Much of that commerce funnels through only nine West Coast ports: Seattle, Tacoma, Portland, Oakland, San Francisco, Los Angeles, Long Beach, San Diego, and Hueneme. Even though twenty-four ports line the U.S. East Coast, more than 40% of U.S. container shipping enters through L.A./Long Beach.[20]

Images of container ships waiting outside of U.S. ports dominated newscasts recently. Even in the best of times, inefficiency has plagued U.S. port capacity. Out of 351 world ports, the Port of Los Angeles' efficiency ranks 328, while Long Beach clocks in at 333, behind port operations in Dar es Salaam, Tanzania, and San Pedro in the Ivory Coast.[21]

Supply chain experts blame such pitiful efficiency rankings on numerous factors: long-term underinvestment and underdevelopment of infrastructure, a lack of data-sharing among supply chain participants, and a union contract that bans fully automated ports.[22,23]

Zoning restrictions also hamper capacity. For example, the Port of Long Beach normally restricts stacked containers to a maximum of two, although officials temporarily upped that limit to four.[24] These same containers routinely stack ten to twelve high on ocean-crossing ships.

Either way, once manufacturing in Asia rebooted after shutdowns in early 2020, U.S. ports have proven incapable of handling the load, and long-term infrastructure investments, by their very nature, take time.

Short-term measures, like mandating that ports operate around the clock, will have minimal effect. Those are Band-Aids, not insights or strategic changes. First, ports would need to train more longshore workers or require overtime, which would create OSHA violations. Then, the other links in the end-to-end supply chain, transport, and warehousing would need to scale up to match.

Drayage, or short-term hauling of containers from the dock to storage in or just outside the port, is a major problem. Every drayage job takes about an hour; then, truckers must get back in line and wait to get reloaded. Independent truckers will take a long-haul, fourteen-hour job over that any day. Press reports quote many truckers complaining about extended wait times at the inefficient U.S. West Coast ports, giving truckers even more incentive to avoid drayage.

Optional pricing could be a temporary solution, at least for those shippers willing to pay to get high-value goods unloaded quickly. When Shari and I cruised through the Panama Canal years ago, I was shocked at how many ships waited at anchor while our cruise ship passed through. The cruise ship lecturer let us know that cruise ships, which have to keep tight schedules, drop $60,000 apiece to speed through the canal. Other container ship owners willing to wait their turn in line paid about $5,000.

Perhaps owners of some of those ships waiting off the U.S. West Coast might pay twelve times the going rate to get their cargo unloaded. Such a move would at least be a real-life strategy change and the beginnings of Insightful Leadership.

Solutions are needed to improve the drastic plunge in global shipping reliability. Before COVID-19, oceangoing freight made their schedules 70% to 80% of the time. In 2021, that number went from speed-surfing to paddleboarding, ranging from 33% to 40%.[25]

Outside of the water, surging demands in consumer goods and shortages in labor and transportation equipment delayed deliveries and skyrocketed logistics costs.[26] Supply chain operators had trouble finding truckers, dock workers, warehouse personnel, delivery drivers, and every other human being needed to get goods from the ports to nearby stores or buyers' doors. Even FedEx and UPS, two huge cogs in the

U.S. supply chain, were so overwhelmed that they suspended deliveries for numerous companies in 2021.

Back in China, it's the Eastern version of the Wild West. Companies will have a $15,000 contract to load a container on a ship. Someone else will offer the shipper $20,000 for that spot. Your container gets left on the dock, and you have no recourse.

All the turmoil led the world to realize how important supply chain operations are for everything you buy, consume, and live with. Consumers took notice. Newscasters offered commentary. Business press, from *Business of Fashion* to *Forbes* to the *Los Angeles Business Journal*, started recommending adding supply chain expertise to the C-suite.

And the C-suite noticed.

Equilar and *Fortune* reported that eighty-five Fortune 500 companies now have a chief supply chain officer or someone with a title filling a similar role, up from seventy-one a few years ago. Companies from startups (eyeglass e-tailer Warber Parky) to Fortune 500 mainstays (Raytheon and Nordstrom) added such roles to their boards.[27]

Perhaps they were noticing what successful companies like Apple (industrial engineer/CEO Tim Cook) and GM (CEO Mary Barra previously held responsibility for the car company's global purchasing and supply chain) knew: without solid supply chain operations, your company, economy, and life will go nowhere.

The insights supply chain specialists deployed were multifaceted, from diversifying inbound logistics to different sales and marketing strategies to flattening peak demand.

On the inbound logistics side, some large U.S. retailers—Home Depot, Target, and Walmart among them—have chartered their own container ships. While this guarantees delivery to the U.S., chartering a ship that carries four thousand containers instead of buying space on one that carries eighteen thousand containers results in less bang for your buck.

Sure, Target's revenue is way up, but they're paying a fortune to execute their supply chain operations, meaning profit margins have declined. Making more money by spending even more money is not a recipe for profitable growth, but it is a recipe for survival and making sure your customers have something to buy.

Chief supply chain officers can also help boards of directors find solutions for the madness that is Black Friday. For many retailers, 30% of their business takes place between November 25 and December 25.

Historically, businesses have thrown their hands up in anguish, saying, "The customer is going to buy when the customer is going to buy."

Demand shaping is an Insightful Leadership marketing/sales strategy that no longer accepts that constraint, because such a heavy load in such a short time hampers a supply chain's ability to perform. For pre-COVID-19 supply chains, the Christmas rush might start stocking the pipeline of goods in July or August, where consumer products, apparel, and other holiday fare sits until getting pushed to the retail location the last month or so of the year.

Before the Disruptions of the last few years, that wait was deemed acceptable. But the explosion of the eCommerce Tipping Point had snarled supply chains to the point where businesses genuinely worried that they would not be able to deliver Christmas in 2021. So retailers aimed to flatten out demand throughout the latter months of 2021.

Rather than waiting around to deliver huge order numbers from their inventories, supply chains sought to prod consumers to make purchasing decisions well before Black Friday and Cyber Monday.

Demand shaping uses marketing that plays off the news of supply chain woes along with the traditional marketing tactic of FOMO (fear of missing out): order early, or your kids won't see presents under the Christmas tree this year; 10% off for the month of September; buy-one-get-one-free sales; and so on.

Like some post-COVID-19 Insightful Leadership solutions, pushing Black Friday earlier in the year was a Paradigm Shift that had been tested before. A couple dozen retailers held Black Friday sales intermittently in July since Amazon started Prime Day in 2015,[28] but it never pummeled into the public's consciousness like day-after-Thanksgiving shopping.

But in 2021, supply chain woes were on top of everyone's mind, especially worried consumers, and deploying holiday sales and promotions earlier in the fall worked: U.S. consumer spending rose 0.6% in September 2021 and 1.4% in October 2021.[29] Mastercard reported that holiday sales from Nov. 1 to Dec. 24, 2021, increased 8.5% from the year before—a 10.7% increase compared with the pre-COVID 2019 holiday period.[30] The November-December 2021 holiday season shopping grew 14.1% from 2020 to a record $886.7 billion, with online and non-store sales growing an additional 11.3% at $218.9 billion.[31]

Earlier Black Friday was also brought to you by expanding Distributed Logistics. Distributed Logistics, where major warehouses and distribution centers push inventory closer to the customer in smaller fulfillment centers, was growing before COVID-19. I myself built and sold a Distributed Logistics company before the pandemic struck.

Complete Distributed Logistics networks will be required to satisfy consumer demand for quick and cheap delivery from now on. Another requirement? Digital Supply Networks, which integrate artificial intelligence, machine learning, and cloud computing to provide end-to-end visibility into supply chain issues—and actionability to solve those issues. You can find more information on Distributed Logistics in Chapter 8 and Digital Supply Networks in Chapter 9.

Of course, like port capacity limitations, politics sometimes get in the way of efficient supply chain operations.

Every county south of St. Lucie, Florida, has banned the

construction of new warehouses. This has the effect of banning Distributed Logistics, making deliveries to Miami and Fort Lauderdale slower and more expensive than final mile deliveries in Atlanta.

The combination of lockdowns and the eCommerce explosion, exacerbated by labor woes, government restrictions, reduced transportation capacity, and rapid shifts of supply and demand, sent supply chains beyond their breaking point over the last two years.

Although some analysts predict supply chains will return to normal this year, I believe they will not be fully repaired until 2023, if not 2024. And that's only if the Russia-Ukraine war winds down and China doesn't launch a military assault on Taiwan. We also have to see if inflation hampers increasing supply chain infrastructure and operations. Then, in a world where Disruption is the new normal, expect more Disruptions beyond that.

As we will see, the great Tipping Points of lockdowns, eCommerce, and broken supply chains have led to huge Paradigm Shifts in how we live, shop, work, and deliver goods and services in the future.

These are Paradigm Shifts that Insightful Leaders must surf through in the future all while looking out for the next waves of Disruptions, Tipping Points, and even newer Paradigm Shifts.

---

1. "The Health Risks of Big Wave Surfing." *Surfertoday*, 30 Oct. 2013, www.surfertoday.com/surfing/the-health-risks-of-big-wave-surfing.
2. "Brad Norris Survives 3-Wave Hold-Down At The Right." *Surfline*, 2 Aug. 2018, www.surfline.com/surf-news/bradley-norris-survives-three-wave-hold-right/31328.
3. Mainali, Miraj. "Lights-Out Manufacturing: Still a Moonshot or a Closer Reality?" *Lux Research*, 21 July 2021, https://www.luxresearchinc.com/blog/lights-out-manufacturing-still-a-moonshot-or-a-closer-reality.
4. Sava, Justina Alexandra. "Change in Remote Work Trends Due to COVID-19 in the United States in 2020." *Statista*, 16 Feb. 2022, www.statista.com/statistics/1122987/change-in-remote-work-trends-after-covid-in-usa/.

5. Mateyka, Peter J., et al. "Home-Based Workers in the United States: 2010." *U.S. Census Bureau*, Oct. 2012, www.census.gov/library/publications/2012/demo/p70-132.html.

6. Parker, Kim, et al. "How the Coronavirus Outbreak Has–and Hasn't–Changed the Way Americans Work." *Pew Research*, 9 Dec. 2020, www.pewresearch.org/social-trends/2020/12/09/how-the-coronavirus-outbreak-has-and-hasnt-changed-the-way-americans-work/

7. Leonhardt, Megan. "COVID isn't the thing keeping people working from home anymore." *Fortune*, 1 Apr. 2022, fortune.com/2022/04/01/remote-work-from-home-march-jobs-report-covid/.

8. Maas, Steve. "Work from Home Likely to Remain Elevated Post Pandemic." *The Digest, National Bureau of Economic Research*, Jun. 2021, www.nber.org/digest-202106/work-home-likely-remain-elevated-post-pandemic.

9. Molla, Rani. "How Remote Work Is Quietly Remaking Our Lives." *Vox*, 9 Oct. 2019, www.vox.com/recode/2019/10/9/20885699/remote-work-from-anywhere-change-coworking-office-real-estate.

10. Parker, Kim, et al. "COVID-19 Pandemic Continues To Reshape Work in America." *Pew Research*, 16 Feb. 2022, www.pewresearch.org/social-trends/2022/02/16/covid-19-pandemic-continues-to-reshape-work-in-america/.

11. Parker, Kim, et al. "How the Coronavirus Outbreak Has—and Hasn't—Changed the Way Americans Work." *Pew Research*, 9 Dec. 2020, www.pewresearch.org/social-trends/2020/12/09/how-the-coronavirus-outbreak-has-and-hasnt-changed-the-way-americans-work/.

12. Morrow, Allison, and Anneken Tappe. "How Millions of Jobless Americans Can Afford to Ditch Work." *CNN Business*, 7 Jan. 2022, www.msn.com/en-us/money/markets/how-millions-of-jobless-americans-can-afford-to-ditch-work/ar-AARPZDb?ocid=entnewsntp&pc=U531.

13. Smith, Morgan. "Expect 'Huge Battles' Over Working From Home Between Employees and Bosses Soon, Says Stanford Professor Who's Studied Remote Work for 20 Years," *CNBC*, 7 Jan. 2022, www.cnbc.com/2022/01/07/stanford-professor-expect-huge-battles-over-working-from-home-soon.html.

14. "Survey: As Workplaces Reopen, 42% of Workers Fear Getting COVID." *The Conference Board.* 21 Aug. 2021, www.conference-board.org/press/return-to-work-survey.

15. Harrigan, Fiona. "The Pandemic's Economic Impact Includes More Americans Starting Their Own Small Businesses." *Reason.com*, 6 Jan. 2022, www.reason.com/2022/01/06/the-pandemics-economic-impact-includes-more-americans-starting-their-own-small-businesses/.

16. "New Business Insights: 2022 Projected to be Another Record Year For New Business Starts." *QuickBooks*, 13 Dec. 2021, www.quickbooks.intuit.com/r/inspiration/new-business-insights-dec-2021/.

17. Parker, Kim, et al. "How the Coronavirus Outbreak Has–and Hasn't–Changed the Way Americans Work." *Pew Research*, 9 Dec. 2020, www.pewresearch.org/social-trends/2020/12/09/how-the-coronavirus-outbreak-has-and-hasnt-changed-the-way-americans-work/.

18. "Quarterly Retail E-Commerce Sales 1st Quarter 2022." *U.S. Department of Commerce*, 19 May 2022, www.census.gov/retail/mrts/www/data/pdf/ec_current.pdf.

19. Kay, Grace. "Kohl's Says Its Amazon Partnership Has Drawn in 2 Million New Shoppers, a Third of them Millennials." *Insider*, 2 Mar. 2021, www.businessinsider.com/kohls-amazon-partnership-2-million-new-shoppers-millennials-2021-3.

20. Wilkie, Christina. "White House Plan Aims to Help Key West Coast Ports Stay Open 24/7 to Ease Supply Chain Bottlenecks." *CNBC*, 13 Oct. 2021, www.cnbc.com/2021/10/13/supply-chain-biden-backs-running-west-coast-ports-24-7-to-ease-bottlenecks.html.

21. "The Container Port Performance Index 2020: A Comparable Assessment of Container Port Performance." *The World Bank*, 2021, www.maritimes.gr/images/PORTS/Container-Port-Performance_Index-WB-2021.pdf.

22. Tirschwell, Peter. "New Data Reveals Berth Inefficiency of US ports." *Journal of Commerce*, 20 Sep. 2021, www.joc.com/port-news/new-data-reveals-berth-inefficiency-us-ports_20210920.html.

23. Morley, Hugh R. "Tentative ILA-USMX Master Contract Bans Full Terminal Automation." *Journal of Commerce*, 14 Aug. 2018, www.joc.com/port-news/longshoreman-labor/international-longshoremen%E2%80%99s-association/tentative-ila-usmx-master-contract-has-terminal-automation-ban_20180814.html.

24. "Long Beach Limits Rules on Container Stacking To Ease The Backlog Of Cargo Ships Waiting To Unload." *CBS Los Angeles*, 22 Oct. 2021, www.losangeles.cbslocal.com/2021/10/22/long-beach-eases-rules-on-container-stacking-to-ease-the-backlog-of-cargo-ships-waiting-to-unload/.

25. Murphy, Alan. "Schedule Reliability Continues to be Under 40% in 2021." *Sea-Intelligence*, 27 Dec. 2021, www.sea-intelligence.com/press-room/113-schedule-reliability-continues-to-be-under-40-in-2021.

26. "U.S. Department of Transportation, Bureau of Transportation Statistics, Transportation Statistics Annual Report 2021." *U.S. Department of Transportation*, 12 Jan. 2021, www.bts.gov/sites/bts.dot.gov/files/2022-01/TSAR_FULL%20BOOK-12-31-2021.pdf.

27. Wahba, Phil. "From Obscurity to Superhero: Chief Supply Chain Officer is Now the Toughest Job in the C-suite." *Fortune*, 10 Nov. 2021, www.fortune.com/2021/11/10/chief-supply-chain-officer-c-suite-jobs/.

28. McGrath, Kristin. "Black Friday in July: History and Statistics." *Blackfriday.com*, 19 July 2021, https://blackfriday.com/news/black-friday-in-july-history-and-statistics.

29. "Consumer spending." *U.S. Bureau of Economic Analysis*, 2021, www.bea.gov/data/consumer-spending/main.

30. The Associated Press. "Despite Supply Issues and Omicron, Holiday Sales Rise 8.5%." *Politico*, 26 Dec. 2021, www.politico.com/news/2021/12/26/holiday-shopping-christmas-omicron-526155.

31. "NRF Says 2021 Holiday Sales Grew 14.1 Percent to Record $886.7 Billion." *National Retail Federation*, 14 Jan. 2022, www.nrf.com/media-center/press-releases/nrf-says-2021-holiday-sales-grew-141-percent-record-8867-billion.

8 PARADIGM SHIFT: DISTRIBUTED LOGISTICS, REQUIRED FOR FUTURE SUCCESS

The Tipping Points of lockdowns, eCommerce and broken supply chains created Paradigm Shifts that accelerated history. In the world of supply chain, those Paradigm Shifts upended the science of inventory, forced companies to suspend deliveries to customers (Chapter 7), and made Distributed Logistics and final mile networks necessities, not nice to haves. Distributed Logistics prepositions inventory closer to customers, allowing enterprises to deliver goods fast and cheap. Final mile, as the name alludes to, gets those goods to the customer's front door, not the corner store down the street. B2C and B2B are increasingly surfing into a new paradigm—B2ME.

Let's say Liliana, a hypothetical executive chef based in Florida, faced a quandary unique to the year 2020.

COVID-19 had shut down in-person gatherings, curtailing Liliana's paycheck and crimping her side business of cooking classes for people who, like her, suffered from gluten sensitivity or celiac disease.

Luckily, sixteen people had signed up for Saturday's

hastily designed online cooking course. Two courses a month and COVID-19 rental assistance could tide her over without making her raid her savings or retirement funds.

But with all the talk on TV of broken supply chains, she wondered if she could deliver 16 different orders of food and event supplies to sixteen different addresses in time.

For her restaurant's gluten-free menu, she had been ordering supplies from the Mama Eleonora All-Natural Pasta Conglomerate in Napa Valley, where she vacationed years ago. Unbeknownst to Liliana, Mama Eleonora had joined and heavily invested in a Distributed Logistics consortium to ensure timely deliveries—well before the Disruptions of the last few years. So had Party Decorations by Theresa, where Liliana routinely ordered décor.

Despite the Disruptions, both businesses promised her two-day delivery when she logged on Wednesday, just enough time for Saturday's class.

All sixteen clients received their gluten-free rigatoni; organic pasta sauce; free-range beef meatballs; green, white, and red bunting; Italian flags on six-inch sticks; and historic Italian placemats with a visage of Guiseppe Garibaldi, the Italian republican revolutionary. Liliana even ordered an Italian flag to hang as a backdrop in her St. Petersburg, Florida kitchen.

The cooking class was a smash hit, and Liliana has continued them. As the world moves beyond the pandemic into the Disruptions of the future, she discovered a geographically dispersed but growing clientele that yearned for gluten-free cooking, yielding more revenue from her side business.

Digital innovation has allowed her to disseminate that knowledge without forcing everybody to drive to her restaurant in St. Petersburg on the Florida Gulf Coast. Now that she is back in her restaurant on the weekends, she orders the supplies for her Monday night cooking classes on Thursday. Distributed Logistics delivers the goods.

Even before the Disruptions of the last few years turned

eCommerce from a growing phenomenon to a Tipping Point, Distributed Logistics enabled such deliveries millions of times a day and hundreds of millions of times a year.

In our world of perpetual Disruption, using smaller warehouses to preposition inventory closer to dense populations, the hallmark of Distributed Logistics, is a Paradigm Shift.

Yes, Distributed Logistics existed before COVID-19, and many Insightful Leaders had specified that necessary shift and started building or, in the case of smaller enterprises (not the Walmarts and Kohls and Targets), joining multi-enterprise Distributed Logistics systems in a race to keep up with Amazon, the Distributed Logistics king. But now, Distributed Logistics is table stakes for any enterprise that wants a chance to stay on its surfboard, play the retail game, and successfully ride the waves of Disruptions-Tipping Points-Paradigm Shifts.

Distributed Logistics networks use forward stocking points to push inventory closer to customers, positioning the enterprise to wait for a simple online click to fulfill all of the customers' retail or brand desires. Deploying this inventory forward gives your enterprise a less expensive, quicker delivery—and it's an integral business strategy that, as Amazon has proved, drives growth.

Beyond Amazon, other enterprises have correlated faster delivery with increased sales. It is not uncommon for brands to see sales skyrocket 15% the first six months after adding same-day delivery from their stores.

COVID-19, the mother of the mother of the mother of all Disruptions, has simply accelerated that trend away from the mammoth 500,000-square-foot (or larger) warehouses serving entire countries or continents. That obsolete paradigm is as useful as a surfboard in a hurricane.

For years, the science of inventory, consolidation, economic order quantity, total delivered cost, and other tools called for those humongous distribution centers to rule supply chains. Such tools and distribution centers work well for minimizing operational expenses, facility costs, and transportation spending, but they do not provide rapid delivery.

Instead, they resulted in two now obsolete delivery Paradigms: Column A, fast and expensive, or Column B, slow and cheap. These days, customers demand fast from Column A and cheap from Column B. Liliana chose Mama Eleonora and Party Decorations by Theresa because their competitors always tacked on extra shipping charges and could not meet her restaurant's tight delivery timelines.

Yes, we all know shipping costs are baked into the price of every product, but time and again, studies have shown that a line item labeled "shipping costs" sends the average American consumer away on their surfboard to another wave, and you lose the sale. It's kind of like how buy-one-get-one-free advertisements always outperform 50%-off sales. Yes, they're the same price, but they drive entirely different consumer behaviors.

The shift toward Distributed Logistics, as with many things in today's eCommerce landscape, started with Amazon. The online behemoth was peering around these corners years ago, spending the quarter-century preceding 2020's pandemic building a Distributed Logistics network anchored by dozens of distribution centers—the big, old kind that supply chain managers spent decades consolidating—that feed hundreds of smaller fulfillment centers, delivery stations, supplemental centers, return centers, and even Whole Foods grocery stores.[1]

These smaller sites, including a fifty thousand-square-foot fulfillment center that opened in Manhattan during the 2014 holiday season, are closer to high-density urban areas.[2] In fact, Amazon now has at least twelve warehouses in the five boroughs of New York City and more than two dozen warehouses in the suburbs surrounding the city. At the time of this writing, no other large competitor had a single warehouse in the city. New York City warehouses can fulfill orders 20% cheaper than those originating in New Jersey.[3]

Amazon's logistics replicate those savings across the country, serving customers faster and cheaper and driving return orders, customer satisfaction, brand loyalty, and growth. If you don't believe it, check Amazon's stock price since its inception.

There are a few reasons for Amazon's success. First, closeness equals inexpensive when it comes to deliveries. No matter what kind of air shipping discount you can negotiate, two-day ground transport from Atlanta to Florida will always be cheaper than flying that product in from Napa Valley, California. Coupling lower shipping prices with inventory proximity also makes it easier to deliver next-day or same-day orders, whether the pull signal comes from a customer or one of your retail stores. Additionally, ground transport beats air any day when it comes to sustainability and carbon dioxide emissions, and returns can be processed or consolidated into a central processing system more rapidly and efficiently at the local level.

Moreover, the pull signal allows your entire supply chain to decide stocking requirements based on demand flow instead of holding huge inventories of safety stock. Your system can rapidly increase or decrease delivery volume to replenish stores or fulfill consumer desires.

Altogether, the Distributed Logistics system offers higher levels of customer satisfaction, a strategic Paradigm Shift that Amazon has mined to the T to skyrocket its sales. Quicker and more affordable delivery equals happy customers equals customer satisfaction equals increased sales.

With this eCommerce Paradigm Shift, people in the couch and chair business would ideally locate their brand's production site in their customer's living room—talk about quick shipping!

That, of course, is not possible. But Distributed Logistics gets you close enough.

If you're in North America, your network can be as simple as a second distribution center on the other coast. A company with one site in Chino, California can benefit from a second distribution center in New Jersey. That will be enough to deliver two-day shipping to 68% of North America's population.

Regional competitors can operate large distribution centers that feed a handful of smaller fulfillment centers. Engineering same-day fulfillment across a national or continental network might take several years and require dozens of distribution centers feeding even greater numbers of smaller fulfillment centers, but the payoff is ultimately worth it. Both options allow you to push inventory closer to your urban population densities, shortening delivery times.

Like all logistics solutions, your enterprise can build this network out on your own, outsource it, or take a hybrid approach. A truly national strategy will likely require a hybrid. Outside of the largest entities—the Walmarts, Home Depots, Kohl's, and other companies worth billions of dollars —no one enterprise has the capital or operational expertise to build and deploy this insight from the ground up.

Beyond capital costs are the traditional supply chain operational concerns: will the brand pile up too much inventory at certain nodes, requiring us to give discounts to clear the network's channels? Will the retailer stock too low and lose sales?

Unlike supply chains of yore, however, today's logistics specialists have better forecasting tools and flow models. Demand planning, real-time data, and even machine learning and artificial intelligence can put the right stock at the right place at the right time. Within fulfillment centers, better technology, better systems, and better automation move that inventory more quickly and accurately than the human hands of yesteryear.

A strategic Paradigm Shift to that same system can benefit brick-and-mortar retail stores. Rapid replenishment keeps site inventory lean, reducing the $100-per-square-foot footprint in favor of $15-per-square-foot fulfillment centers. The closer your inventory is to your customer, the closer you can forward deploy to those large urban areas.

Outside of your warehouses and fulfillment centers, you'll have to catch the wave and ride the final mile to your customers' residences.

The final mile, the last bit of distance that delivers goods or services to the end user, tends to be complex and costly. Amazon built its networks with the final mile in mind, while FedEx and UPS were engineered to deliver B2B (such as multiple packages from Office Depot to, well, an office), not B2C (sending single parcels to houses, condos, and apartments).

FedEx and UPS designed their business models to pick up fifty parcels from one business, move them to a hub for sortation, and deliver those parcels to fifty different businesses. However, the hub groups deliveries from multiple businesses together, so at each business, a FedEx or UPS driver drops off three, five, eight, ten parcels or more—one from vendor A, one from vendor B, one from vendor C, and so on.

The U.S. Postal Service was conceived with the final mile in mind. But its original mission called for delivering letters, not bulky packages. Post offices nationwide have efficient automation to handle letters, but unlike letters, magazines, and flyers, oversized parcels don't fit into the little mail slots at the post office. Even the USPS's mail trucks are too small to handle the growth in package demand. Couple that with the fact that over the last few decades, email had siphoned off much of the postal service's letter volume, which was its bread and butter, and you have a recipe for losing money.

So the only one of the original big three kahunas in U.S. shipping designed with the final mile in mind cannot efficiently deliver the package volume the eCommerce explosion demands.

And as the disruptive waves of the last few years swept eCommerce into a Tipping Point regarding how consumers shopped for goods, the final mile has become even more important. This Paradigm Shift into Distributed Logistics has your enterprise asking UPS or FedEx to deliver desktop computer accessories to an office's seventy-eight employees... at their residences, not the office complex. Or, in the example of Liliana, they're delivering cooking supplies and décor to multiple discrete customers instead of Liliana's restaurant. Multiply that by millions of deliveries per day, and B2B is looking more like B2C or, as I have dubbed the new Paradigm, B2ME (business-to-me).

For the three biggest logistics services in the United States, B2MEs are money losers. Yet that share of the delivery market is growing, as shown by Amazon, which now delivers more packages per day than FedEx. Eventually, Amazon will surpass UPS and deliver more than any other shipping service.

Of the 2.4 million packages (up half a million since COVID-19) delivered daily in New York City, more than 80% end up with residential customers. That number compares to 40% before the outbreak.[4]

The B2ME Paradigm is less profitable than B2B for many reasons. Delivery density is substantially less; drivers who used to drop off five to ten boxes at each location now average 1.2 boxes per delivery site, and their trucks travel longer distances, taking more time.

Even before the pandemic, FedEx and UPS had added various fees to make up the difference: residential surcharges, additional handling fees for packages that do not fit in their normal systems, surcharges for extra-large packages, and surcharges for delivering to rural areas, among others.

Inefficient eCommerce packaging slices B2ME profits even more. Fulfillment centers aren't going to operate with cardboard boxes of forty-five different sizes; they'll have a big box, a medium box, and a little box. That little box which is, say, 6 x 6 x 2 inches, might only hold one computer mouse for delivery.

Peering around corners and looking at the growth of eCommerce and how it was drowning their bottom line, carriers introduced dimensional weight in 2015, where parcels are charged based on how much weight they expect a 6 x 6 x 2 inch box to hold. Since UPS and FedEx traditionally charge by weight, a truckload full of 6 x 6 x 2 inch boxes full of goods that weigh roughly four ounces each was a pure profit plunger.

Besides the weight and size of the products, they still had to deal with the final mile, often the most expensive part of the journey. So, UPS and FedEx partnered with the U.S. Postal Service to handle final deliveries. However, the U.S. Postal Service now delivers more parcels than letters, and it still cannot make money. In many areas, those final miles are handled by couriers who used to deliver contracts and documents before the advent of e-signature services.

In fact, Chris, a contractor for McFeely Speedy Delivery Services, delivered several of Liliana's packages around the St. Petersburg area.

Like many in the digital era, Chris has been forced to wear many hats. Online e-signature services like DocuSign and PandaDoc have largely eliminated courier services for contracts, drawings, and other documents. Beyond delivering medical specimens, there just wasn't much work left for Chris —until eCommerce stepped in. He recognized the Paradigm Shift and developed a new strategy for his workflow. Unlike you, the leader of a startup or an enterprise, Chris, a sole proprietor, did not have to communicate his plans or gain alignment from partners to deploy his insight.

Now, depending on the day of the week, time of year, and time of day, Chris switches between hauling medical specimens and eCommerce packages for McFeely Speedy Delivery, dropping passengers off for Uber or Lyft, and serving food via Uber Eats or DoorDash.

For McFeely Speedy Delivery, Chris is one of two thousand independent contractors who either work part-time for a delivery service or two or who use the freedom and flexibility of choosing between services to make delivery a full-time job, often working ten-plus hours each day.

On Mother's Day weekend, when flower deliveries increased sixfold, Chris worked three fourteen-hour days, then took the next three days off. But his hard work and knowledge of the local delivery market has him earning $100,000 annually.

Final mile providers like McFeely have grown in the eCommerce era and exploded in the wake of COVID-19.

Sure, if you're shipping from Los Angeles to Chicago, you are going to use UPS, FedEx, or the U.S. Postal Service. They're your only choices.

But if you're shipping from Los Angeles to Huntington Beach, Fullerton, or Pomona, you're going to use a local Californian or regional courier. It makes no sense for FedEx to take a box from Los Angeles up to its regional hub in Oakland and deliver it right back to the L.A. area.

These couriers are where the eCommerce Tipping Point drives the Paradigm Shift of smaller warehouses that preposition inventory closer to population densities. These smaller warehouses accommodate the growth of online ordering and the decline in retail store sales—Distributed Logistics and the final mile.

This service offering is designed for B2ME. Because of eCommerce, there are many more deliveries, and because of Distributed Logistics, these deliveries are not traveling as far.

How people shop for and receive their goods are two towering Paradigm Shifts in today's world of retail delivery. In fact, the shift from brick-and-mortar retail to online shopping to the necessary omni-channel presence that offers consumers both options—there's that optionality I've been recommending again—is humanity's biggest change in getting food and sustenance since we left hunter-gatherer status.

Insightful Leaders must navigate the waves of the Paradigm Shifts of Distributed Logistics and final mile delivery to handle growing online sales, declining store sales, and smaller warehouses pushing inventory closer to population density, all while making sure that consumers in all channels are happy.

1. "Amazon Global Supply Chain and Fulfillment Center Network." *MWPVL International Inc.*, 2021, www.mwpvl.com/html/amazon_com.html. Accessed 14 Oct. 2021.
2. Rubin, Ben Fox. "Why Amazon Built a Warehouse Inside a Midtown Manhattan Office Tower." *CNet*, 21 Dec. 2015, www.cnet.com/tech/services-and-software/why-amazon-built-a-warehouse-inside-a-midtown-manhattan-office-tower/.
3. Haag, Matthew and Winnie Hu. "In New York, as shoppers went online, Amazon went on a warehouse-buying spree." *The New York Times*, 4 Mar. 2021, www.nytimes.com/2021/03/04/world/in-new-york-as-shoppers-went-online-amazon-went-on-a-warehouse-buying-spree.html.
4. Haag, Matthew and Winnie Hu. "In New York, as shoppers went online, Amazon went on a warehouse-buying spree." *The New York Times*, 4 Mar. 2021, www.nytimes.com/2021/03/04/world/in-new-york-as-shoppers-went-online-amazon-went-on-a-warehouse-buying-spree.html.

9 PARADIGM SHIFT: RIDING THE NEXT WAVE WITH DIGITAL SUPPLY NETWORKS

As supply chains broke down across the globe, CEOs wanted to know what was going on. That Tipping Point accelerated chief supply chain officers into the path of history, earning them respect, promotions, and media scrutiny. With that respect, they were charged with adding resilience to corporate operations to handle the Paradigm Shift of how we live, work, learn, and shop. Forward-thinking supply chain officers know that with Disruption as the new normal, they need to complete the decades-long evolution of supply chain to a phase where complex networks of multiple enterprises have complete visibility and actionability along their entire end-to-end supply chain—Digital Supply Networks. Without this innovation, your enterprise will suffer.

In the year 2020, as COVID-19 and lockdowns ravaged the globe, I, James A. Tompkins, Ph.D., founder of fifteen companies, writer and contributor to more than thirty books, recipient of fifty-plus awards for service to his profession (including the prestigious Frank and Lillian Gilbreth Industrial Engineering Award from the Institute of Industrial and Systems Engineers), became legitimate.

In March, locked down with my family at our North Carolina beach house, I was working in my fourth-floor office, a domain rarely breached by others.

In fact, I don't even think my wife of fifty-three years had ever come up and sat in my office. But at the end of March 2020, Shari Tompkins did just that.

I thought, "Oh wow, what did I do now?" I figured I must have screwed up in some way.

She smiled at me and said, "Congratulations."

"Well, thank you, but what did I do?" I asked.

"You are now legitimate," Shari said.

"Well, my mom and dad never told me," I replied. "I never questioned that!"

Shari explained that for our decades of marriage, she had described my profession to her friends, my friends, our children, and our grandchildren.

And still, no one had a clue what I did for a living.

"But for the last four nights on the evening news, they're talking supply chain, supply chain, supply chain," Shari said. "So now all my friends go, 'Oh, that's what Jim does.'"

And all of a sudden, I am now credible. I now have validity.

"We Cannot Make a Thing" Triggers Respect

In a world where Disruption is the new normal, supply chains and supply chain managers have become valid in more eyes than just those of my wife, her friends, and my family.

Because in 2020, supply chain was the tidal wave devouring the surfboards of enterprises and entrepreneurs worldwide, ripping old paradigms out with the tide right and left.

As COVID-19 moved from country to country, with industries and transport alternately locking down and opening back up, leaders and managers struggled to fill demand that skyrocketed in some sectors. Most supply chains lacked the Digital Supply Networks to bring end-to-end visibility to problems way upstream, much less the actionability necessary to do something about such problems. They did not conduct sufficient environmental scanning, did not peer around corners, did not even imagine that paradigms could change.

When the CEO of a home appliance company sees revenue decline, he calls in his Chief Operating Officer (COO) to find out why. The COO explains that two refrigerator plants are closed.

The CEO asks, "Why? With COVID, everybody's staying at home. They're eating at home. They want to buy extra refrigerators or bigger ones. What the heck is going on?"

"Boss, I can't make the refrigerators because I can't get compressors," the COO replies.

The CEO wants to know why the COO can't get compressors, which are made in Brazil. Unbeknownst to the CEO, the parts that make the compressors come from China, and China, in early 2020, was closed—the twelve to thirteen-week shutdown covered in Chapter 5.

The CEO, seeing that he is substantially missing his budget and knowing that demand is out there for other products, tells the COO to start making washing machines. The problem is that the COO can't start manufacturing washing machines, even though they're domestically made, because the motors come directly from China.

"Boss," the COO sadly says with a shake of his head, "I've looked at every single product we have, and we cannot make a thing."

Sure, the compressors didn't come from China, and the washing machines may have been domestically made, so the C-suite and the people in its environs expected no problems. Unfortunately, it's rare to find a manufactured good sourced from only one country. Parts and raw materials hail from all around the world, with many originating in Asia. Even parts that don't originate in Asia often use raw materials or subcomponents from China.

All of a sudden, the C-suite population realizes that it needs supply chain insight into what they're doing.

Since COVID-19, supply chain professionals estimate that their representation on boards of directors and elevation to chief supply chain officers have increased tenfold. The mention of "supply chain" on quarterly earnings calls increased 50% in 2021 from 2020, which held the previous record.[1]

So after nearly three decades as a defined practice (the term "supply chain" entered our vocabulary in the early 1990s), COVID-19 brought supply chain professionals respect. COVID-19 surfaced troubling issues with our current non-resilient supply chains that made it beyond the boardroom and impacted consumers, ranging from material and product shortages to supply chain Disruptions to the rising cost of goods sold.

In the ideal world of just-in-time manufacturing and supply chain, enterprises don't stockpile raw materials, parts, and other inputs. These things just get in the way and cost money to store and maintain.

The resulting cost reductions helped supply the world with affordable goods, an absolutely marvelous current state—until Disruptions changed that state.

The second Disruptions hit, operators start closing plants, and businesses start disappointing customers.

And that's what happened.

So these days, everybody, from philosophers at the corner bar to soccer moms to garage band members to twenty-four hour cable news broadcasters, is discussing and passing themselves off as experts on supply chain.

Resilience, the Price of Respect = Digital Supply Networks

No advancement comes without punishment. With the newfound respect the C-suite has for supply chain, it wants chief supply officers to build resilience.

Resilience is the final phase of what I call EERR—efficiency, effectiveness, respect, and resiliency.

When logistics professionals coined the term "supply chain" in the early 1990s, the entire concept was cost reduction, the industrial and systems engineering concept of efficiency, the first "E" in EERR. They applied supply chain strictly to internal corporate operations: the planning people talked to the sales people who talked to the procurement people who talked to the manufacturing people who talked to the distribution people.

Kimberly-Clark's supply chain pros didn't necessarily examine the world of their raw materials beyond getting them inside their doors for production. If they did, it might have only been a step or two beyond their organization. Once truckloads of toilet paper and other products were at the Hyatts, office complexes, or Safeways, their concerns ended.

Internally, manufacturers and supply chain pros looked to reduce delivery times, production times, missed deliveries, transportation costs, inventory, and the like to increase efficiency and reduce what they view as the costs they control. But as you will grow to understand, Digital Supply Networks will allow you and your network partners to control costs well beyond your organization's doors. This enables improvements to links upstream that gather your product's initial inputs and downstream to your end user, massively reducing the cost of goods sold across your end-to-end supply chain.

The second E, effectiveness, starts when multiple organizations use visibility to start working together. Your supplier says, "I'm going to have a supply problem on this particular product."

So you tell your supplier, "How about making this other

product instead? As a matter of fact, this alternative product is hotter in the market right now, so make even more."

This collaboration also involves customers. Retailers let their suppliers know, "We're going to have a sale on women's dresses and men's formalwear." In turn, suppliers can plan for those increases in volume.

By 2005, most progressive supply chains started acting on the realization that better customer service could increase sales. Get it to them faster, wrap it up nicely, put their name on the envelope, put their name on the shirt—if I can conduct some value-added activity and give customers additional value, my effectiveness will go up, and my revenue will go up, too.

Efficiency and effectiveness, the "EE" in EERR, lasted all the way up to 2020. The world's supply chains, broken by the combination of work-from-home, shop-from-home, the eCommerce explosion, and geopolitical and financial crises, had CEOs looking for the cavalry (or maybe lifeguards to protect them from the great white shark of COVID-19) in the form of their newly anointed Chief Supply Chain Officers.

Respect, in this case, is not about ego. Instead, respect concerns how organizations invest their money and how they listen to what's happening inside the organization.

That investment should build the aforementioned Digital Supply Networks—an artificial intelligence and machine learning-powered chain that links your raw materials, no matter where their genesis is, all the way to your output's end user, no matter how many links down the chain that final customer resides.

Deploying Digital Supply Networks is the only way to achieve that second R in EERR—resiliency.

Resiliency will become all the more important in an era marked by potentially crippling inflation. The 7% inflation rate from 2021[2] could drop to 6.3% this year,[3] but I think it will actually go in the other direction, marking thirty months of revenue that may look good on paper but, in reality, are worth millions of dollars less, not to mention the extra cash flow needed for raw materials, logistics services, maintenance, labor, land, technology—everything your business requires.

Investing in Digital Supply Networks may give your enterprise the competitive advantage to surf through the Disruption of inflation. Leaders will have real-time, end-to-end supply chain knowledge to have the option of changing prices dynamically at the individual or single-transaction level, continually adjusting the company's projections and product mix.

The ability of an enterprise's supply chain to change prices dynamically has an overwhelming impact on margins and cash flow.[4] The data generated from these systems allows for continuous adjustments to the company's projections and product mix, all huge competitive advantages at a time when knowing what the customers can and are willing to pay for is more essential than ever before.

A supply chain is simply the sum of every action trading partners make to source, produce, and deliver customer satisfaction. While a great supply chain will have numerous optimized links, a fully enabled Digital Supply Network will:

- handle high degrees of complexity,
- eliminate latency with real-time information,
- autonomously resolve many problems with artificial intelligence and machine learning,
- optimize the entire chain, not just specific links,
- and harvest the benefits of internal and external synergies even while facing VUCA.

Digital Supply Networks will require two components: 1) information technology that connects all enterprises with a single version of truth, and 2) a spirit of teamwork and cooperation.

Even within a single enterprise, getting multiple departments and locations to cooperate for the common good has been historically difficult. Siloed behavior is the rule, not the exception.

Digital Supply Networks take on the additional problem of cooperation between enterprises. Some companies have hundreds or even thousands of suppliers for their various components, and goods get distributed to thousands of locations across the globe. But beyond convincing all partners to adopt common goals and agree that harmony yields better results than discord, multiple enterprises must figure out a way to orchestrate operations across multiple networks to forge one seamless end-to-end supply network.

For eons, businesses have waxed and waned between vertical integration and distributed networks. Vertical integration, characterized by Henry Ford's River Rouge Complex in the early 20th century, essentially brings supply chain and operations under one roof or one company, everything from raw materials to the finished product. Leaders and managers manually oversee operations, making decisions close to where the work is done. Vertical integration offers lower transaction costs, lower uncertainty, and synchronization of supply and demand within your operations.

On the other hand, Adam Smith presented the benefits from specialization and economies of scale in his 1776 book *The Wealth of Nations*. That paradigm is the backbone of the modern manufacturing and supply chain world, with far-flung networks stretching across all major continents. Specialization, global supply chains, and manufacturing operating via economies of scale are the reasons why the Walmarts, Targets, Kohl's, and Amazons are usually chock full of goods affordable to virtually every family above the U.S. poverty line.

Digital Supply Networks impart the best of both worlds: distributed operations and vertical integration. There are specializations and efficiencies inherent in distributed operations; the best tire maker makes the tires, the best fender maker makes the fenders, the best steering wheel maker makes the steering wheels, and they all come together in a car.

Henry Ford's idea of vertical integration, on the other hand, includes involvement where leaders and managers can keep an eye on things and make sure they are optimal (back in the day) or optional (what you need to survive in the future).

The obvious, inherent problem is synchronizing supply and demand among numerous countries, manufacturers, and suppliers, all operating with separate management and leadership teams. Beyond each product's global suppliers and distributors, a consortium of enterprises could be dealing with hundreds of thousands of orders and tens of thousands of stock keeping units, or SKUs.

However, with Digital Supply Networks, you don't have to merge every corporation and government into one Whole World Behemoth Inc. The technology and cooperation inherent in Digital Supply Networks remove boundaries between supply chain links. Such visibility reveals issues in real time along your end-to-end supply chain, which encompasses every link, from raw material to finished product, no matter which corporate roof that component hangs its hat under.

Digital Supply Networks include one database and one user interface, one version of truth among all suppliers, carriers, customers, manufacturers, and distributors. Capacities, constraints, and bottlenecks are dealt with at the network level, not in individual silos or nodes. An optimal solution across the entire network is a better option than an optimal operation at the silo level.

Plans and reality merge so that planning and execution become one function, not two.

Exponentially Reducing Cost of Goods Sold

For the past few decades, many business experts have described the business world as a competition of supply chain versus supply chain, not enterprise versus enterprise. But in a world dominated by Digital Supply Networks, the biggest savings will come from reductions in your cost of goods sold—what you pay your vendors, including the inventory and transportation costs of your vendor, and their vendor, and their vendor, and their vendor. This moves the cost of goods sold well beyond your enterprise's borders.

Thus, the new age of free market capitalist economics could be a much more cooperative paradigm than the old model where you compete with other enterprises, even penalizing your suppliers for real or perceived failures.

If you hurt your suppliers, you hurt yourself. If you benefit your suppliers, whether they're one step away from your process or fourteen suppliers down the chain, your entire end-to-end supply chain is more effective.

If you have five, eight, eleven, or fifteen different corporations combining to drive out waste and costs along the end-to-end supply chain, the massive reduction in your cost of goods sold accumulates not just to you but to your customers. This is a key competitive advantage in an era where inflation is rearing its ugly head for the first time in decades. The bottom-line impacts can be exponential. The ability to drive costs from an enterprise's entire supply chain—not just optimize a few links here and there—will keep the end product or service affordable for your customers. Your non-digitized competitors will not be able to compete.

Therefore, Walmart's on-time in-full program (OTIF) is abominable. The massive retailing company penalizes suppliers based on their percentage of on-time and in-full deliveries. That, of course, is the exact opposite of reducing your costs. Walmart, a highly respected retail and logistics operation, is pursuing the exact opposite of the Digital Supply Networks required by the future.

Maybe Walmart isn't surfing the right waves because the visibility and actionability needed to make Digital Supply Networks a reality were not possible until the year 2017.

By 2010, cloud computing had advanced to the point where managers and leaders could achieve visibility throughout their end-to-end supply chain. But just because they could see the problem didn't mean they actually had any options.

However, by 2017, other technological advances—particularly in machine learning and artificial intelligence—brought actionability to the table. Now, they can see and fix the issue at hand, quickly repairing or replacing the chomped-on surfboard.

With the right investments and know-how, your supply chain can work as one seamless unit, an end-to-end Digital Supply Network linking manufacturing, logistics, and supply chain into a whole, unveiling problems and deploying fixes in real time.

Real-time blind spots have always hampered supply chains. Digital Supply Networks can resolve those operational issues at the operational level, leaving you free to tackle the future.

Remember, Disruption is the new normal, and it can come from innovation (how Amazon sparked the growth of online retail) or disaster (natural or manmade). The year 2020 saw the confluence of multiple Disruptions from both avenues.

Think back to the Ever Given container ship stuck in the Suez Canal. Businesses waiting for parts from India kept calling the trucking company they worked with. The trucking company kept saying, "Yes, the parts are coming, but the ship from the Netherlands is not here." But the containers with those parts never made it to Rotterdam; they were stuck in the Suez Canal on a separate ship, several links away. Unknowingly, the trucking company was lying to its customers. A Digital Supply Network would have given the trucking company's management the knowledge that their delivery was stuck in the Middle East, allowing them to deploy other options.

Those things happen often, and just as often, businesses are guilty of trying to solve network problems with enterprise software. By definition, a network consists of multiple enter-prises, so software designed for one enterprise will never solve a network problem.

At best, it will add visibility about the link in front of you and the link behind you, but not in real-time mode and certainly not end-to-end.

So if you're looking at the link for the truck that's supposed to come from Los Angeles to Salt Lake, you're not going to know that your 3PL's truck won't receive the container off the ship in the Port of Long Beach because the container never made it onto the ship out of China in the first place.

So while your 3PL's truck arrives at the port to pick up your container—just like your enterprise software said it would—your container remains on the dock in China.

The key is network visibility. The real-time problem-solving power of Digital Supply Networks, which gives opera-tions personnel visibility into problems and automated solu-tions driven by machine learning and artificial intelligence, adds that network actionability.

While artificial intelligence and machine learning can automate solutions to many link problems throughout your Digital Supply Network, the network's AI would escalate something like the Ever Given to human decision makers.

Sure, you can't get the ship out of the Suez Canal or the container off the dock in China, but knowing the issues early on allows you to pursue and deploy different options.

Such resiliency will complete the evolution of supply chain into Digital Supply Networks I first envisioned with my 2003 book *No Boundaries: Break Through to Supply Chain Excellence,* which outlines a mode of supply chain operations I wanted even before the term Digital Supply Networks existed.

A Company at War vs. Synergistic Cooperation

No Boundaries shook up the supply chain world and encouraged enterprises and entrepreneurs to look beyond their doors. My theory that the path to supply chain excellence had six phases gave birth to the concepts of end-to-end supply chain and the supply chain evolution from efficiency to effectiveness to respect to resiliency, although it took me another seventeen years to coin the acronym EERR.

Phase one, business as usual, is when everything is, well, screwed up. The finance people hate the sales people. The sales people hate the production people. Every silo in your company is trying to be the best silo instead of optimizing the entire operation. The company is at war—a civil war.

Sadly, in a lot of enterprises, this is the normal state of affairs.

In phase two, link excellence, the different parts of the company start to work together, bringing visibility to the supply chain—at least internally. Sales and operations planning were big steps toward link excellence, and could indeed be considered its genesis. Enterprises had one set of numbers, one forecast, and everybody knew they were going to march to that drum along their internal supply chain.

In phase three, visibility, organizations start to look outside their doors for the first time. What happened before the raw materials hit the loading dock? What happened to my supplier? What happened to my customer? Visibility could be considered the first step away from an organization toward the end-to-end supply chain. Phase three mainly acts as an early warning system. Enterprises can more easily plan for sales increasing or decreasing or how to adjust if a supplier is not going to deliver a product on time. Although professionals were peering beyond their doors, their thinking was still internal; by understanding what happens before inbound logistics gets to the door and what happens after outbound logistics leaves, they can make their links better, reducing transportation and inventory costs.

Phase four, collaboration, paired partnerships with technology to accelerate visibility beyond the doors to meet marketplace demands.

This started happening around 2005, so looking back, phase four is when the supply chain started moving toward EERR's second E, effectiveness.

In phase five, synthesis, imagine a multi-enterprise supply chain as a big chain traveling over a hot flame. Each chain has a different color: your internal supply chain links are blue, inputs from various suppliers are red and green, and outputs to multiple customers are purple, pink, and yellow. This flame of synthesis is so powerful that it melts the chain, and you have a flow of molten metal.

Now, the product flows from the raw material, through production, and all the way to the customer. Your overall supply chain increases its return on assets, maximizes inventory turns, minimizes obsolete inventory, improves customer satisfaction, reduces costs, and achieves an integrated supply chain.

Phase five is the stage where your Digital Supply Network gives you complete visibility from you to your supplier. From your supplier to the trucking firm. From the trucking firm to the L.A. port. From the L.A. port to the port in China. From the port in China to the supplier in China, to that supplier's supplier, to that supplier's supplier.

Phase six is velocity, which you're able to achieve closer and closer to real time. Complex entities create multilevel networks that use a combination of partnerships, flexibility, robust design methods, demand planning, and agility to meet the needs of the marketplace.

The end-to-end supply chain inherent in achieving this means that enterprises large and small see their product from the advent of their raw materials several suppliers down, through distribution to their corporate customers, and all the way to the customer who walks out of Kroger with a twelve-pack of paper towels.

So phase six saw the need for today's Digital Supply Networks years before the technology existed to achieve that state. Now, your Digital Supply Network allows visibility into any problems along that chain. Artificial intelligence and machine learning handle many of these issues automatically, only escalating serious complications that have no automated solutions to human decision-making.

Achieving resilience with velocity and Digital Supply Networks far surpasses achieving resilience the easy way—having your just-in-case analysts build huge inventory stockpiles.

Huge inventory stockpiles cause your CFO to go berserk. And there's conflict, so much conflict that enterprises might as well go back to my phase one of supply chain evolution—business as usual, or a company at war with itself. That's what many commentators are advocating for when they call for a return to the past. It's a return to huge inventory stockpiles.

However, with every Paradigm Shift, the solutions involve doing something different. Instead of returning to war, enterprises need to realize that the term supply chain, after being quite useful for nearly three decades, is obsolete.

Coming from me, who has worked in and talked about supply chain for as long as the term has existed, it's a difficult but necessary admission.

To continually handle Disruptions, Tipping Points, and Paradigm Shifts in the future, enterprises and entrepreneurs need to replace their supply chains with a Digital Supply Network.

Finance is the overriding factor that makes or breaks every enterprise. Stock prices, earnings per share, and related measures such as free cash flow are the things that keep the C-suite up at night.

I contend that in a world where Disruption is the new normal, operational and supply chain drivers such as cost of goods sold, cash-to-cash cycle, length of time between order and delivery (total supply chain time), gross operating margins, and quality will be the main value creators that affect an enterprise's overall finances.

Efficiency, effectiveness, respect, and resiliency will bring together decades of operational improvements to synergize a Digital Supply Network between trading partners, delivering heightened financial benefits to each partner. Minimizing the cost of goods sold and total delivered cost (TDC) is the path to greater gross operating product margins for all.

This is where Insightful Leadership must have vision— the vision to realize that an assemblage of optimized links does not beget a Digital Supply Network. Executives and entrepreneurs must realize the importance of harvesting the benefits of internal synergy (transportation, inventory, and other costs) and external synergy (cost of goods sold and customer satisfaction) even while facing perpetual Disruption.

For supply chain and manufacturing, this is truly the Insightful Leadership Paradigm Shift of our time. The Tipping Points have already passed, the Paradigm Shifts are here, and the strategy for deploying innovations that will replace obsolete supply chains with Digital Supply Networks is ready. It's time for you to communicate to your teams and organizations, gain alignment with your partners, and deploy Digital Supply Networks, giving you visibility and actionability so you can ride the next wave of Disruptions, Tipping Points, and Paradigm Shifts instead of floundering in the surf.

Keys to Digital Supply Network Success

Network, synergy, harmony, and orchestration are the four keys to Digital Supply Network success.

1. **Network:** A chain consisting of links all connected from one to the other. The chain's performance constraint is the weakest link. A

network has many connections of links. Instead of being measured by one link, network performance is measured by the synergy across network elements. Links work together, develop synergy, and have enough resilience to adjust around weak links. The more the links work together, the better the network will perform. Remember, with Disruption as the new normal, you will not be able to optimize each individual link anymore. Instead, the network must identify the weak link in real time and know what alternatives can be pursued to resolve any problems. Resilience does not eliminate Disruptions, but it does have the ability to identify and resolve the impacts from those Disruptions.

2. **Synergy:** The output from the whole exceeding the output of its parts. Links that operate for the best interest of a network create stronger synergy than links that work for a single entity's best interest. This bigger picture of working for the whole network comes from the harmony of the links.

3. **Harmony:** Links which understand that what is best for the network is best for them. Harmony only occurs when all work together as one, marching to the same beat.

4. **Orchestration:** Using information to guide performance. Orchestras combine sheet music, a conductor, and scores of individual musicians to create harmony. Without a conductor using the information from the sheet music to guide performance, there is noise, not harmony. Likewise, the Digital Supply Network requires information to harmonize, a difficult proposition when you're talking about hundreds of suppliers and logistics providers dealing with frequent

Disruptions. You must use the tools of orchestration.

Turning these four keys together will result in a supply chain engine that has the power to handle high levels of complexity, a real-time network that eliminates latency, and autonomous resolution tools (artificial intelligence and machine learning) that enable orchestration.

---

1. Boyle, Matthew. "'Supply Chain' Mentions on Earnings Calls Hit a Record High." *Bloomberg News*, 13 Oct. 2021, www.bloomberg.com/news/articles/2021-10-13/supply-chain-chatter-hits-record-highs-on-earnings-calls. Accessed 20 Oct. 2021.
2. Pickert, Reade. "U.S. Inflation Hits 39-Year High of 7%, Sets Stage for Fed Hike." *Bloomberg News*, 12 Jan. 2022, www.bloomberg.com/news/articles/2022-01-12/inflation-in-u-s-registers-biggest-annual-gain-since-1982.
3. Payne, David. "Inflation Will Ease, But Only Gradually This Year." *Kiplinger*, 11 May 2022, www.kiplinger.com/economic-forecasts/inflation.
4. Charan, Ram. "Leading Through Inflation: How Sales & Marketing Must Transform." *Chief Executive*, 1 Mar. 2022, chiefexecutive.net/leading-through-inflation-how-sales-marketing-must-transform/.

10 PARADIGM SHIFT: SORRY BOSS, YOUR OFFICE IS DEAD TO ME

Enterprises the world over are faced with a Paradigm Shift in how and where we work, a shift that often excludes the office. Employees have seen the benefits of working from home and realize they're more productive. They wonder why they must add that hour-long commute back to their day. Insightful Leaders must handle strategic decisions involving office space investment, workforce geography, remote-hybrid work options, and more, cognizant that a displeased workforce can surf away to better opportunities or start their own enterprise. Power has clearly shifted from management to labor.

When COVID-19 shut down the Lone Star State in March 2020, a ten-person Texas-based nonprofit association expected it would return to the office shortly, just like much of the world believed. As time meandered and they adjusted to working remotely, leadership and the board had the foresight to take stock of all the changes and Disruptions they had faced.

They scanned their environment. Their staff was successfully working from home, making it less viable to spend valuable capital on rent. They did not need office space to welcome in tons of visiting customers. Even with social distancing, masking, and other precautions in place, returning to the office still exposed their staff to health risks, not to mention the inconvenience and discomfort of wearing masks in common areas. And who knew what Disruption would come down the pipe later, sending everyone scurrying back home?

This process of peering around the corners developed the insight that their office was an obsolete paradigm. Their Insightful Leadership strategy involved ditching their expensive lease when it came up for renewal in fall 2020.

The move worked. Freed from a hiring pool limited by geographic location, they could competitively recruit from anywhere in the country and grow their staff at a time when many were laying people off. The association hired its first two non-Texas employees in August 2020—one in New York and one in Virginia—and soon followed with a hire from California and another from Utah.

Now, the nonprofit uses work-from-home technology to increase its effectiveness and efficiency with a staff that lives in four different time zones. The staff is happier; the association is productive and growing. Everybody wins.

This is the type of Insightful Leadership needed to deal with the work-from-home Paradigm Shift, which has swept into a tidal Paradigm Shift dubbed the Great Resignation. Whether it's because more baby boomers have chosen early retirement, people in service jobs have grown tired of poor pay and treatment, or your former workforce has struck out on their own and become nascent entrepreneurs themselves, power has clearly shifted from management to labor. You will be faced with strategic decisions involving everything from workforce geography and composition to office space investment to when (or whether) to return to the office to use of overtime to leadership style to increasing productivity without killing innovation. All the while, you will be cognizant of the fact that if you displease your workers, they can surf away to better opportunities—or start their own enterprises.

Pre-COVID, about 17% of the U.S. workforce worked remotely full time.[1] At COVID's peak, 61% percent of the U.S. workforce worked remotely, a staggering increase.[2]

Even more impressive has been remote work's staying power. After the pandemic, some experts have predicted that somewhere between 20%[3] and 70% of workers will "clock in" remotely, either full-time or multiple days a month.[4] As of June 2022, two full years after COVID-19 shut down the world, most say that 25%-35% of the U.S. workforce is working remotely.[5] Their eCommerce B2B deliveries will head to their home addresses; think of UPS or FedEx delivering loads of printer paper, computers, and peripherals to dozens or hundreds of separate locations instead of one central office.

The numbers might not spike to 61% again in the next few years, but they will grow.

Even if the remote workforce stabilizes at "only" 25% post-COVID, that's still a B2C (or B2ME, as I dubbed it in Chapter 8) market that has substantially grown from the pre-COVID-19 17%. Conversely, those workers no longer generate as much demand on the B2B side of the ledger. We've already seen what that does: just remember the great toilet paper search mentioned back in Chapter 5.

A one-third increase or decrease of sales in any category is a Paradigm Shift. Think of the sales categories that drop and the demands that increase when people work from home. Businesses would have to reconsider demand for power lunches, day care/nannies/babysitters, shipping office products to the office, and after-work cocktails, among others. On the other hand, more people will be buying casual wear and groceries they will cook at home. They will ship office products and home computers directly to their homes. And more moms and dads will coach soccer.

You should apply your environmental scan to your thinking along with the fact that remote work will surely grow —a year from now, the 25% will be 26%; two years from now, we'll be at 29-30%. Those insights could pop ideas into your head about future Tipping Points that will lead to Paradigm Shifts in and around your business sector.

For example, when my wife and I recently dined at a swank New York City restaurant, the maître d' wore a suit and tie. But there was not another suit, tie, or sport coat in the place. Before COVID-19, all men, including me, would have worn at least a sport coat and dress shirt, while many would have the full uniform of suit and tie. The women at the restaurant were also dressed down. Most, like Shari, wore slacks and sweaters, not dresses.

The next day, *The Wall Street Journal* featured an article discussing how the lockdown Tipping Point has resulted in a Paradigm Shift in dress—we no longer feel the need to dress up and be fancy. Insightful Leaders in the apparel industry needed to use this knowledge to cope with the potential growth of leisurewear and athletic gear as well as the decline of business suits and ties.

So, what is the future of the workplace?

Well, a Conference Board survey found that only 4% of U.S. workers want to work exclusively in the office, while 20% want to work remotely full time.[6] There were more than 67% in the "hybrid" category. Based on worker preferences, hybrid could be the winning category for a solid and reliable labor force.

However, this greatly varies due to the expectation that "normal" will return and offices will fill up again. COVID-19's Delta variant ended that consensus, and Omicron upended it further. By the end of Omicron, fewer than half of U.S. office workers were back in the office, and many companies pushed their timelines later.[7]

Add to that the realization that your workforce might not like the office as much as you do.

As many companies were telling their employees they must be back in the office full time by a set date, Disruptions kept pummeling those plans. By then, more workers were defining new paradigms and responding with a revised sociology of life by saying,

"Yeah, have a nice day. I quit. I know I've been with the company fourteen years, but I'm gone. I want to find a place where I can work remotely because I kind of enjoy going to my son's baseball game and my daughter's soccer game, and I can't do that when I work at the office."

It's the reverse of *Atlas Shrugged*, the 1957 Ayn Rand novel that imagined a world where top-level men and women, the movers and the shakers, go on strike. These days, leaders and managers face difficulty recruiting those at the other end of the entrepreneurial spectrum: servers, cooks, retail staffers, truck drivers, warehouse personnel, dock workers, etc.

Many workers are finding more attractive wages and working conditions elsewhere. And after all, they're asking, if they're "essential" workers, why is their pay so low compared to non-essential personnel who have the privilege and option of working from home?

On that front, more North American companies are opening up to the possibility of remote or hybrid options. Out of its roughly 55,000 U.S. employees, PricewaterhouseCoopers allows about 40,000 client-facing workers to live anywhere in the continental U.S. Employees may still be required to visit a client site or the company office occasionally. Compensation is based on their geography, so those moving to lower-cost living areas saw their salaries drop.[8]

Facebook, Zillow, and more are offering more workers remote or hybrid options. As more workers flock to those remote or hybrid options, the lockdown Tipping Point (the one that begat the work-from-home and accompanying changed sociology of life Paradigm Shifts) has forced leaders and managers into new strategies in how they hire and operate. Insightful or not, leaders of any size of organization are not competing for talent in a geographic pool within driving distance of the workplace—they are competing worldwide.

Enterprises that take a hard line and require their staff to be in the office five days a week are going to cost themselves good employees, and the employees that stay and "take it" could be less qualified staff. Your older workers might not even need to look for new opportunities. As I've mentioned several times, skyrocketing stock portfolios and home values have many of them taking the retirement option.

From 2008 to 2019, about one million U.S. residents aged 55 and older retired each year. In 2020 and 2021, the total of those numbers topped 3.5 million.[9]

Hundreds of thousands of others are leaving their current gigs to become their own bosses as consultants, retailers, and small-business owners.[10]

All of these changes are adding additional opportunities for those formerly stuck below to move into better positions, either at their current company, in another enterprise, or by striking out on their own.

Others, like my friend Dmitri, are firing their bosses and moving on. When his boss protested that Dmitri was the only person challenging the organizational status quo, Dmitri responded that that was why he was leaving.

"I cannot deal with the fights I have to go through to get things done," Dmitri told his soon-to-be former employer. "Some things should be as easy as slicing butter, but it's like I'm trying to slice a diamond."

Losing an employee—or several—can severely disrupt an organization's operations. Many companies are using overtime to solve worker shortages, relying on current employees to log more hours.

The average manufacturing worker went from 2.8 hours of overtime a week in April 2020 to 4.2 hours of overtime a week in August 2021. The extra pay might be nice (and adds to your payroll costs), but the added stress and burnout, not to mention the time spent away from family, means more workers leave.[11]

The vicious cycle increases the pressure on workers who remain. So, over time, overtime costs.

On the other hand, some employees prefer working in the office. The economic shutdown limited childcare options, so during COVID-19, home workers who had to double as parents often faced a difficult juggling act during the workday, adding to their daily stress levels.

Just like different beaches have different wave categories that wax and wane with the tide, different regions will present different issues. Overall, Canadians are less likely than U.S. workers to say they prefer remote work. Only 4% of Canadians worked remotely pre-pandemic, a rate that did grow to 30%. Younger Canadians seem to have more interest in returning to the office, whereas those 55 and older prefer remote work.[12]

Insightful Leaders have other ways of riding the wave of this Paradigm Shift to future success. Virtual teams are growing, but "traditional teamwork problems such as conflict and coordination can escalate quickly in virtual teams."[13]

Insightful Leaders will need to develop and communicate a strategy with guidelines, non-task interactions to build teamwork, formal team processes, and team goals to mitigate conflict. It's possible that a more communal orientation in moral decision-making, higher sensitivity to risk (particularly about health issues), higher conscientiousness, and more attentive communication styles can be effective in crisis management.

Companies may also look to save money by replacing full-time employees with remote contract workers. Many prefer the flexibility of contract work, especially if they can pick a lower-cost geographic region to live. Others would resent not having benefits, particularly healthcare and access to a 401k.

Whatever you decide, it's clear that in many instances, leaders spent years being, well, rather dumb in requiring everybody to be in the office, and my concept of optionality would easily help with proper workforce allocation.

Depending upon the enterprise, you might want to establish a fully remote workforce or a hybrid solution. Some who prefer to work remotely could do so while others could choose to be in the office every day, or perhaps leaders could set up a rotation where employees are in the office some days and remote the other days (more on this in Chapter 13).

After all, not everybody who had the chance to work remotely liked it. And remote work during the shutdowns would likely be different from remote work going forward. Pandemic remote work was a surprise, done on the fly with little preparation. It just happened. The pressures of childcare, cabin fever, and Zoom overload took their toll.[14]

This means remote work outside of the pandemic could also be even more attractive than remote work during the pandemic. The pandemic stress of remote work can ease when the occasional office day replaces Zoom meeting after Zoom meeting after Zoom meeting, and parents can stay at their "home" desk without having to care for children who have since returned to school or daycare. So, again, hybrid grows as an option.

Many consulting, accounting, and service firms are discovering this. Particularly in consulting, a large number of employees work remotely, living at their clients' job sites three to four days a week.

That halted during COVID-19—clients were not going to continue to allow people access to job sites during a pandemic driven by aerosol transmission of a virus, particularly since the employees being consulted weren't at the site, either.

Frankly, it really, really knocked a number of consultancies on their keisters because they didn't know how to work and consult remotely.

Perhaps they had a couple of videoconferencing machines, but they weren't used well. Often, in the beginning, consultants wound up with the old speakerphone in the middle of the desk—a decidedly 20th century solution to a 21st century problem. *Popular Science* was reporting on how speakerphones helped busy executives carry on conversations "without lifting a finger" back in the 1940s.[15]

Many consultants had never heard of Zoom or Microsoft Teams, so the shift to the new remote working tools was a major, major, major change, a Paradigm Shift that, in many cases, will not revert back to consultants consistently traveling to client sites multiple times a week.

Personally, I have found remote work twice as productive. I'm not spending four nights a week on the road, hustling from car to airport to taxi to Uber to Lyft to subway to limousine. I'm not walking up and down halls, going to meetings, making small talk with office mates.

Others may be different, but I can schedule video meetings and calls from 7 a.m. to 5 p.m. Preparing for the day requires about two or three hours the previous night reviewing notes and news reports of my clients' companies, looking at LinkedIn profiles, and developing agendas and talking points.

Personally, I have enjoyed a greater quality of life despite the workload. I don't have to leave home; spending four nights a week in an airplane, while it sounds exotic and exciting, gets old after years and years. The travel grind drains you. When you get home on the weekend after you've been in the air all that time, you fall on the bed and sleep for ten hours. It's just not physically healthy.

So while businesses have touted life-work balance for years (with some actually offering it while others only paid lip service to the concept), a new family-first perspective has been uncovered from the employees' viewpoint. Moms and dads discovered that they liked being home and watching their children's soccer games and making chocolate chip cookies together. This mindset will result in more permanent work-from-home scenarios.

People of the more nomadic set will become, well, digital nomads, working from a third place. Their "office" might be the local library, coffee shop, beach house, cruise ship, an apartment in Argentina, a hostel in Australia—anywhere with high-speed internet.

While Starbucks invented the concept of working in a third place, the digital nomad concept was first envisioned in 1997.[16] For years, the sector was defined by independent workers such as freelancers, independent contractors, and the self-employed. In mid-2020, COVID-19 work-from-home (or at least work-away-from-the-office) mandates exploded the "work from anywhere" population from 7.3 million to 10.9 million people in the United States, a nearly 50% increase from 2019.[17]

Some forward-thinking companies are letting their entire staff—not just C-suite execs—work remotely.[18] The results? The digital nomad cohort that held down traditional jobs (not influencers or travel writers Instagramming photos from the beach) nearly doubled from 3.2 million in 2019 to 6.3 million in 2020. Even *Harvard Business Review* has articles detailing how your organization needs a digital nomad policy.[19]

Current thinking limits these remote work opportunities to a select few: those who deal in information, technology, consulting, communications, creative services, and those who produce goods and services that translate into the digital realm (think papers, reports, computer code, digital advertising, blogs, and more).

However, a McKinsey and Co. report maintains that more than 60% of the U.S. workforce will not have opportunities to hold employment without going to the job.[20] After all, there's no way a remote workforce could operate a factory that produces, say, machine tools, right?

Not so fast.

Telefacturing, a semiautomated manufacturing concept that uses telerobotics and co-robotics concepts, could expand the work-from-home paradigm to the manufacturing set. Telefacturing workers would remotely operate "fabrication machinery, assembly cells, material handling equipment (such as pick-and-place manipulators, lift trucks, etc.), quality control and testing equipment, packaging and warehousing and other manufacturing operations."[21]

Now that we are well past the beginning of COVID-19, reports about the benefits of remote and hybrid work keep pouring in. Three recent studies from Prodoscore, Ergotron, and Owl Labs found upticks in productivity, worker happiness, work/life balance, focus, physical and mental health, and job satisfaction.[22]

Others report that hybrid workers feel more stress, but usually because the bosses still try to control and dictate schedules rather than working in concert with their charges. With Disruption as the new normal, bosses are going to have to give up some of that old-time, top-down control and offer real flexibility.[23]

Clearly, a remote workforce—either completely remote or one established with the optionality of a hybrid solution— offers challenges to leaders, insightful or otherwise.

Still, some bosses fret that remote work can hamper creativity.

One of those bosses is Microsoft CEO Satya Nadella. Microsoft published a peer-reviewed research project in *Nature Human Behavior* that said long-term remote work could threaten collaboration and innovation.

The study's authors wrote that working in solitude, despite the advent of modern communications technology, negatively affects workers' ability to acquire and share information across groups and convey and process complex information.[24]

Other CEOs are also pushing back. Tesla, Google, and Goldman Sachs all have issued return to the office mandates, although some executives consider such requirements tone deaf.[25] Only half of Goldman Sachs' employees returned to the office. Two months later, the investment bank seemed to reverse its directive, giving junior staff extra days off each year and senior staff time away from the office without a fixed vacation day allotment.[26]

Whatever happens in the eternal battle between leaders and labor, the work-from-home Paradigm Shift is one that Insightful Leaders will gain insights from, aim to harness the power of those insights, and develop strategies that their organizations will buy into for quite some time.

---

1. Sava, Justina Alexandra. "Change in Remote Work Trends Due to COVID-19 in the United States in 2020." *Statista*, 16 Feb. 2022, www.statista.com/statistics/1122987/change-in-remote-work-trends-after-covid-in-usa/.

2. Leonhardt, Megan. "COVID isn't the thing keeping people working from home anymore." *Fortune*, 1 Apr. 2022, fortune.com/2022/04/01/remote-work-from-home-march-jobs-report-covid/.

3. Maas, Steve. "Work from Home Likely to Remain Elevated Post Pandemic." *The Digest, National Bureau of Economic Research*, Jun. 2021, www.nber.org/digest-202106/work-home-likely-remain-elevated-post-pandemic.

4. Molla, Rani. "How Remote Work Is Quietly Remaking Our Lives." *Vox*, 9 Oct. 2019, www.vox.com/recode/2019/10/9/20885699/remote-work-from-anywhere-change-coworking-office-real-estate.

5. Leonhardt, Megan. "COVID isn't the thing keeping people working from home anymore." *Fortune*, 1 Apr. 2022, fortune.com/2022/04/01/remote-work-from-home-march-jobs-report-covid/.

6. "Survey: As Workplaces Reopen, 42% of Workers Fear Getting COVID." *Conference Board*, 21 Aug. 2021, conference-board.org/press/return-to-work-survey. Accessed 6 Oct. 2021.

7. Thorpe, Kevin, et al. "Predicting the Return to the Office." *Cushman & Wakefield*, Sep. 2021, www.cushmanwakefield.com/en/insights/predicting-the-return-to-the-office#:~:text=Key%20Report%20Findings%3A,2021%20and%20then%20trend%20lower.

8. Cutter, Chip. "PricewaterhouseCoopers Says Most U.S. Staffers Can Now Live Anywhere." *The Wall Street Journal*, 1 Oct. 2021.

9. Fry, Richard. "Amid the Pandemic, a Rising Share of Older U.S. Adults are Now Retired." *Pew Research Center*, 4 Nov. 2021, www.pewresearch.org/fact-tank/2021/11/04/amid-the-pandemic-a-rising-share-of-older-us-adults-are-now-retired/. Accessed 28 Dec. 2021.

10. Mitchell, Josh, and Kathryn Dill. "Workers Quit Jobs in Droves to Become Their Own Bosses." *The Wall Street Journal*, 29 Nov. 2021, www.wsj.com/articles/workers-quit-jobs-in-droves-to-become-their-own-bosses-11638199199.

11. Weber, Lauren. "Companies Use Overtime to Solve Worker Shortages. That May Cost Them More Workers." *The Wall Street Journal*, 18 Sep. 2021.

12. Thorpe, Kevin, et al. "Predicting the Return to the Office." Cushman & Wakefield, Sep. 2021, www.cushmanwakefield.com/en/insights/predicting-the-return-to-the-office#:~:text=Key%20Report%20Findings%3A,2021%20and%20then%20trend%20lower.

13. Endresen, Janice. "COVID-19's Impact on Work, Workers, and the Workplace of the Future." Cornell SC Johnson College of Business. 25 Sep., 2020.

14. Samuel, Alexander. "So, You Think You've Tried Remote Work? You Probably Haven't." *The Wall Street Journal*, 22 Sep. 2021.

15. Torrone, Phillip. "First Speaker Phone...?" *Make:*, 4 Nov. 2006, makezine.com/2006/11/04/first-speaker-phone.

16. Makimoto, Tsugio, and David Manners. *Digital Nomad*. Wiley, 1997.

17. Everson, Miles, et al. "Your Company Needs a Digital Nomad Policy." *Harvard Business Review*, 12 Jul. 2021, hbr.org/2021/07/your-company-needs-a-digital-nomad-policy.

18. Lufkin, Bryan. "Is the Great Digital-Nomad Workforce Actually Coming?" *BBC*, 15 Jun. 2021, www.bbc.com/worklife/article/20210615-is-the-great-digital-nomad-workforce-actually-coming.

19. Everson, Miles, et al. "Your Company Needs a Digital Nomad Policy." *Harvard Business Review*, 12 Jul. 2021, hbr.org/2021/07/your-company-needs-a-digital-nomad-policy.

20. Lund, Susan, et al. "What 800 Executives Envision for the Postpandemic Workforce." *McKinsey Global Institute*, 23 Sep. 2020, www.mckinsey.com/featured-insights/future-of-work/what-800-executives-envision-for-the-postpandemic-workforce.

21. Khoshnevis, Behrokh. "Telefacturing – a paradigm for the 21st century." *Industrial Engineer*, vol. 47, no. 11, Nov. 2015. *IISE*, www.iise.org/industrialengineer/Details.aspx?id=40115.

22. Robinson, Bryan. "3 New Studies End Debate Over Effectiveness Of Hybrid And Remote Work." *Forbes*, 4 Feb. 2022, www.forbes.com/sites/bryanrobinson/2022/02/04/3-new-studies-end-debate-over-effectiveness-of-hybrid-and-remote-work/?sh=1b81554e59b2.

23. Caminiti, Susan. "Workers Want Hybrid But Say It's Exhausting Them. Here's How Companies Can Fix That." *CNBC*, 8 Feb. 2022, www.cnbc.com/2022/02/08/workers-say-hybrid-is-exhausting-them-heres-how-companies-fix-that.html.

24. Stillman, Jessica. "New Microsoft Study of 60,000 Employees: Remote Work Threatens Long-Term Innovation," *INC*, 20 Sep. 2021, inc.com/jessica-stillman/remote-hybrid-work-paradox-microsoft-satya-nadella.html.

25. Berger, Chloe. "Executives Push Back Against Elon Musk's 'Tone-Deaf' Return-To-Office Ultimatum." *Fortune*, 8 Jun. 2022, fortune.com/2022/06/08/ceos-slam-elon-musks-return-to-office-policy-great-resignation.

26. Gordon, Nicholas. "Goldman Sachs Pushed Staff to Return to the Office. Now the Wall Street Bank Is Giving Executives Unlimited Time Off." *Fortune*, 16 May 2022, www.yahoo.com/video/goldman-sachs-pushed-staff-return-063730538.html.

11 EMBRACING PARADIGM SHIFTS GOING FORWARD

In a world of perpetual Disruptions, Tipping Points, and Paradigm Shifts, organizations must continually innovate to remain successful. Today's world is not about creating a new product every five years and doing continuous improvement. Today, organizations must respond to the work-from-home Paradigm Shift, the digital commerce Paradigm Shift, and the need to replace broken supply chains with Digital Supply Networks. But more important than addressing these three current Paradigm Shifts is building the organization for tomorrow that will foster Insightful Leadership, leadership that continually scans Disruptions, Tipping Points, and Paradigm Shifts to create a continuum of reinvention and innovation that enables your organization to continually ride the waves of these turbulent times.

In 2021, even as the global semiconductor shortage forced many automakers to curtail production and shut down plants, Tesla increased production.

How could Elon Musk's car company ride the Paradigm

Shift of a semiconductor shortage to greater success when every other automotive company couldn't?

Two words: optionality and innovation.

Tesla's electrical and firmware engineering teams took it upon themselves to design, develop, and validate nineteen new variants of microcontrollers to alleviate the semiconductor shortages, which hampered Tesla's factory in Fremont, California, for all of three days.[1]

This is the kind of Insightful Leadership enterprises need in order to continually innovate in a world of perpetual Disruptions, Tipping Points, and Paradigm Shifts. Continual improvements and the creation of a new product every five years is no longer enough. You are going to face Disruption. You will need foresight into those Disruptions to anticipate the upcoming Tipping Points, and you will need insight to develop innovations that ride the new Paradigm Shift's waves to success.

Others can bemoan the Paradigm Shift of the broken supply chain. The federal government can propose billions of dollars in subsidies to jumpstart domestic semiconductor production.

Musk's engineers saw a problem at Tesla and solved it— you know, what engineers are trained to do.

Our team has demonstrated an unparalleled ability to react quickly and mitigate disruptions to manufacturing caused by semiconductor shortages. Our electrical and firmware engineering teams remain hard at work designing, developing and validating 19 new variants of controllers in response to ongoing semiconductor shortages.[2]

FROM TESLA'S SECOND QUARTER 2021
EARNINGS UPDATE LETTER.

Strong, creative engineering teams like those at Tesla give your organization options when it faces obstacles, table stakes when Disruption is the new normal. Others, like Tompkins Robotics, can see Disruption on the horizon and devise new material handling systems to meet the growing market needs of eCommerce—not knowing that the Tipping Point into the next Paradigm Shift, instead of unfolding over years, would hit us like a tsunami.

On the healthcare front, even before the massive Disruptions of recent years, U.S. startups took aim at adding useful technology to an ossified, bureaucratic system that mainly disrupted patients' ability to receive quality care at affordable prices, all while burning out providers via administrative overload.

These are the Insightful Leaders who define obsolete paradigms, develop strategies to replace them, and deploy these insights to continue riding the waves to success.

The issues with healthcare have grown, festered, remained unaddressed, and been exacerbated by COVID-19. Healthcare could be said to be in the Disruption phase, while Tesla has been through the entire cycle of innovating through Disruptions and Tipping Points, creating a Paradigm Shift in the automotive industry.

Stories of innovation abound beyond Tesla's microcontroller-semiconductor issue, which was solved because CEO Elon Musk and his team had the foresight to have a stellar contingent of engineers on staff. Their knowledge led to the insight that allowed Tesla to mostly sidestep semiconductor issues that slowed other auto giants.

Doubted from its inception in 2003, Tesla is now the most valuable automaker in the world and worth more than the next six publicly traded car companies combined.[3]

Tesla's innovations include using new hardware and software architecture (basically, the way you put a car together), investing in and improving battery production, and building out a charging station network for its customers. These handle

potential Disruptions and bottlenecks at the vehicle production level (vehicle architecture), the component level (batteries), and the system level (charging network).

According to the *Harvard Business Review*:

"Tesla's hardware architecture—a flat pack of
batteries at the base, two electric engines (front and
rear), no transmission, etc.—also gives it an advantage
over competing electric vehicles built on traditional
vehicle architectures, such as a lower center of gravity,
greater energy density, and more efficient battery
management. This means that pound-for-pound,
Tesla tends to beat out competitors who try to
leverage parts of the old internal combustion vehicle
architecture, for example, by putting batteries in the
trunk rather than in a flat pack at the bottom."[4]

These insights never would have come out of a traditional
automotive company, one looking for incremental improvements based on the architecture that surrounds internal
combustion engines. But Musk had the foresight to anticipate
that the move toward electrically powered vehicles was not a
fad but a true Disruption that would lead to a Tipping Point,
cresting into a Paradigm Shift. He clearly drives his teams
toward innovation and communicates the necessity of
thinking differently, aligning his teams to ride those insights
toward dominance in the new paradigm—all while continuing
to innovate.

Beyond vehicles, Musk's company has pushed the boundaries of innovation with Powerwalls, its integrated battery
systems, to reduce reliance on the electricity grid; solar roof
tiles; solar panels; and giga-scale megapacks to power energy
projects. By 2021, Tesla had more than three hundred patents

on its various innovations.[5] Despite—or maybe because of—those innovations, critics have long predicted Tesla's imminent bankruptcy and doom. In fact, in 2019, the website Clean-Technica published "A Short History of Tesla Critics' Claims." The thirty-seven item list ended with: "Now there's no doubt about it. Stores are closing and Tesla will finally, really, truly, honestly go bankrupt. Should we restart the Death Watch?"[6]

On the day that story was published, March 4, 2019, Tesla closed at $57.07 per share. Its price has skyrocketed since then.[7]

Along the way, Musk's innovations have revolutionized car production, virtually creating the electric vehicle sales category from scratch, and won fans among customers, investors, and corporate leaders.

Tesla truly has developed a cycle of innovation (more on that in Chapter 12).

We should all aim to handle Disruptions, Tipping Points, and Paradigm Shifts so well.

A Material Handling Revolution

Tompkins Robotics, on the other hand, is more at the Tipping Point stage of its evolution.

Supply chain experts have long said that eCommerce takes five times more resources than replenishing inventory in retail stores. Instead of personnel and machines handling cases and pallets to ship to stores, eCommerce breaks open the cases, selects an item from this case, an item from that case, a couple of items from another case, and consolidates them. The slow shift toward picking and packing those "eaches" instead of cases requires infinitely higher labor content.

In the United States, people outnumber retail stores by more than a 300-to-1 margin. The more-people-than-store ratio means delivering eCommerce to individual residences adds to that labor content, along with the fuel, trucks, and other logistical resources necessary.

For decades, warehouses, distribution centers, and fulfillment centers have consolidated orders and sorted packages to destinations via the same process using some type of loop conveyor system, whether a tilt tray, crossbelt, bomb bay, slide tray, shoe sorter, or pop-up wheel. Even the growing prominence of automated guided vehicles (AGVs) didn't change this much, as they followed predetermined paths throughout the floor plan.[8]

But the advent of autonomous mobile robots (AMRs), such as Amazon's Kiva, caused a wide shift over the last fifteen years. Unlike AGVs, AMRs are not tied to guided tracks, nor are they encumbered by the limitations of fixed conveyorized systems.

Still, the paradigm of warehouse material handling, whether store replenishment, eCommerce, or some combination of the two, remained in the realm of fixed put walls and batch picking, requiring high labor content, whether that labor was human or robotic.[9]

Even pre-COVID-19, some areas, including those surrounding Indianapolis and Memphis, faced tighter labor markets.

Some in the supply chain world, Amazon especially, had the foresight to know that the eCommerce requirement for "each" picking was the wave of the future, a wave hampered by the difficulty of finding and paying for labor.

Years ago, I also had the foresight that the Disruption of eCommerce would reach a Tipping Point. The insight developed from that foresight? That distribution/fulfillment was ripe for an automated, transformative material handling system, one that could handle case picking and each picking and easily transition between the two paradigms.

Propelling that transformation was the genesis behind Tompkins Robotics' 2016 birth. Leaders peered around the corners by garnering feedback from potential customers, revealing that nobody wanted AMRs to operate on a mezzanine that would take a year to build, cost millions of dollars, require regulatory approval, and be difficult, if not impossible, to move.

Company leaders took that insight and worked toward the new paradigm of material handling, just waiting for when eCommerce would hit a Tipping Point. Within a few months in 2017, Tompkins Robotics created a flexible, portable, modular, scalable, and configurable material handling system.

Tompkins' AMRs travel on a single- or multi-story platform, carrying items from induction to order consolidation. Every part of the system—the AMRs and the platform itself—is on wheels. As desired by the end user, fulfillment centers can rearrange a robotic sorter system in a day.[10]

The Tompkins Robotics system beautifully fits in a world where everything, including supply chains (see Distributed Logistics in Chapter 8), is getting more decentralized. A company with one big Atlanta warehouse might decide it can serve regional customers quicker and better (and in the age of eCommerce, quicker is almost always better) by forward-deploying inventory to additional, smaller fulfillment centers in Charlotte, Orlando, and Memphis.

That organization can literally break apart the Tompkins Robotics system in Atlanta; send parts to Orlando, Charlotte, and Memphis; add a few assets to each site; and have four distribution systems deployed to serve the region.

A fulfillment center with four lines can configure one to process returns, one to process outbound shipping for eCommerce, and two to process outbound store replenishment. In the fall, when hungry stores look to stock up for holiday sales, the Tompkins Robotics wheels spin, and the return processing line transforms to handle store replenishment, doubling that capacity to 50% of the fulfillment center footprint. The two eCommerce lines keep humming. When store replenishment demand begins to diminish around November, one store replenishment line transitions to eCommerce, giving the enterprise three eCommerce lines and one store replenishment line.

On January 1, when supply chain systems always face many returns, the warehouse can transition to 50% returns, 25% eCommerce, and 25% store replenishment in a matter of mere minutes.

With the system on multiple levels, it takes up less space. Because organizations don't need permits, your personnel can roll boxes off the truck and hook them together like Lego blocks, deploying a lot faster—and redeploying in hours to meet changing consumer demand.

None of these capabilities exist in traditional material handling systems, making Tompkins Robotics not just a compelling business case and value proposition, but also a Paradigm Shift in material handling, just in time for the eCommerce Tipping Point reached during the COVID-19 Disruption.[11]

Two other Tipping Points are pointing toward that Paradigm Shift: 1) microfulfillment, and 2) automating every step of the process.

The pandemic era's tenfold growth in eCommerce meant labor content exponentially grew as labor supply diminished. Throughout the world's supply chains, fearful employees stayed home or, even worse, fell ill and died. In addition to the lacking labor supply, stimulus payments to consumers skyrocketed overall demand.

Pre-COVID-19, companies were aiming to replace a conveyor-type system with an upgrade, but they still relied on manual labor for induction and takeaway.

You can't find enough people. You're paying a lot more for the people you do find. The turnover in those people is much higher than it has been in the past, so you're constantly retraining them. The Disruptions of the last few years have generated a perfect storm, a Paradigm Shift, on the labor side. Therefore, distribution systems want to automate every possible bit of material handling for order sortation and delivery that they can.

The Tompkins Robotics solutions often save up to 75% of the labor from induction to takeaway. Further innovations in 2022 will remove the labor required to do takeaway.[12]

That automation also perfectly fits with the move toward more microfulfillment centers, which often are closed retail spaces repurposed as miniature warehouses.

When eCommerce was 2-3% of a grocery store's total, each store could handle the volume, whether orders were delivered directly to the consumer's address or consumers shopped online and picked up their items at the store. That "Instacart" model worked well until eCommerce volume topped 8-12%, depending on store location and size.

However, at the height of the COVID-19 pandemic, 40% of grocery store orders came via eCommerce. That volume has dipped back into the 20% range, still well beyond the eCommerce capabilities of most grocery store operations. Even at 20% eCommerce, store aisles were overwhelmed by online orders with professional shoppers and store employees frantically restocking shelves. Adding in contention between the everyday shopper and the professional shopper created friction on the sales floor. Some volumes were too high for stores to turn their back rooms into mini-fulfillment centers, so they turned to the next best thing—that shuttered store five blocks away.

The insight was transitioning these retail spaces, or "dark stores," into microfulfillment centers that might service two to three retail outlets, particularly grocery stores. Microfulfillment centers do not have to worry about shoppers, so their smaller aisles and taller shelves can stock more products without increasing square footage. These higher-density, lower-footprint outlets can ship orders placed online by, say, 10 a.m. to the retail outlets for shoppers to pick up by 3 p.m. while also delivering online orders directly to consumers' residences.

Retail operations had been considering this microfulfillment model for certain high-density areas, such as Southern California, Northern California, Orlando, Miami—maybe ten to twelve areas around the country.

After the Disruptions of the last few years, microfulfillment, a natural evolution of Distributed Logistics that forward-deploys inventory closer to the end user, is all the rage of the supply chain world.[13]

Now, did my team at the nascent Tompkins Robotics know in 2016 that a global pandemic and geopolitical and financial crises would skyrocket eCommerce, that employees working largely from home would drive 40% of grocery orders online, and that microfulfillment would move from a useful model for a few areas to a Paradigm Shift in the world of material handling and product delivery?

No, of course not.

But our environmental scan did foresee that 1) the digital innovation to make such a Paradigm Shift possible was already in place, and 2) eCommerce was growing rapidly. Put those two together, and Disruption was sure to follow. And because of our material handling/warehousing insiders, we had insight into the issues facing the sector and our customers. Therefore, we were ready with Tompkins Robotics to surf the waves of Disruption through the Tipping Point on our way toward success in an entirely new paradigm.

Tesla

The Disruption: Lack of semiconductors.

The Insight: Available microcontrollers, similar to semiconductors, could be reworked to handle semiconductor functions.

The Innovation: The Tesla team designed, developed, and validated new variants of controllers to mitigate ongoing semiconductor shortages.

The Success: While other car companies curtailed production, lost sales, and missed bottom-line goals,

Tesla had a three-day shutdown and actually increased production.

Tompkins Robotics

The Disruption: eCommerce has been steadily growing, and it requires five times the logistical resources of old-fashioned retail store replenishment.

The Insight: For decades, consolidating orders and sorting packages for delivery has been held back by conveyor type systems limited to fixed paths, whether you used forklifts, people, conveyors, or AGVs, but AMRs are not limited to fixed paths.

The Innovation: AMRs on portable platforms can be broken down, reconfigured, moved, and adjusted to meet ever-changing demand.

The Success: Tompkins Robotics is now a highly successful company serving over forty customers; demand grew so much that it had to add shifts and suppliers in the COVID era.

Disrupting Healthcare Toward Success

Even before the COVID-19 Disruption, U.S. healthcare faced mounting problems: a system rife with administrative overload that burned out providers, fragmented care, and long wait times to make appointments. It left many who needed medical services out in the cold.

Add that to the current fee-for-service U.S. healthcare model, where patients and insurers pay providers for visits, tests, interventions, hospitalizations, and so on, and you get a system of, as many healthcare insiders say, "sick care" instead of healthcare.[14]

In most business sectors, technology infusions have increased quality and decreased prices. In healthcare, where it's not uncommon to rely on 20th century fax machines, medical costs continue to increase exponentially. The digital innovation that allowed for the explosion of eCommerce during the last few years has totally bypassed the healthcare system.

Into that maelstrom swirled COVID-19, a Disruption that sank even more healthcare capacity. Lockdowns prevented many medical providers, especially primary care physicians, from seeing patients. Even when offices reopened, many patients feared catching a highly contagious, deadly pathogen.

An estimated 8% of U.S. physicians, an approximate total of sixteen thousand, closed their practices due to the pandemic, and 43% reduced their staff.[15] More providers were bought out or merged with other practices. Other doctors, buoyed by skyrocketing 401Ks and not necessarily relishing close contact with patients in a COVID-19 environment, retired to the golf course.

Emergency rooms and hospitals faced the opposite problem: too many patients, not enough staff. Providers in hard-hit areas were inundated with patient backlogs worldwide.

COVID-19... A Healthcare Accelerator?

For years, medical providers, be they nurses, doctors, or technicians, have complained about burnout. Long hours and high stress often make the high pay not worth it, and it's even worse for those at the lower end of the pay scale.

Change, however, comes slowly in healthcare. While telemedicine tech has been around for most of this century (Skype debuted in 2003), before COVID-19, only 1% of patient-provider encounters came via telemedicine.[16]

As with many things, the Disruption of COVID-19 accelerated virtual care into a Tipping Point. As lockdowns took hold and primary care providers financially struggled, the healthcare monolith moved. Medicare authorities and private insurance companies slowly loosened their rules to pay doctors for telemedicine.

That nascent infusion of digital innovation has started to creep into parts of healthcare, such as the growth of medical wearables (FitBits, smart watches, wearable ECG and blood pressure monitors, and more) tied to the Internet of Things and the expansion of value-based care models (highlighted by Medicare Advantage/Accountable Care Organizations). The same digital innovation could replicate the kind of changes in healthcare—lower prices, higher quality, happier customers—that long ago surfed into the oceans of other economic sectors.

In summer 2020, at COVID's height, telemedicine soared to 70% of provider-patient visits. That has dropped to the high single digits/low double digits and will likely settle in around 5%, healthcare insiders believe.

While it is a large drop from its 70% high, 5% remains a 500% increase from pre-COVID-19 telemedicine, a true Paradigm Shift. Most of that opportunity will show up in what insiders call low-intensity healthcare. This is because the younger population is 1) healthier, and 2) more amenable to using devices. Young people don't get as sick as older patients who often need more personal care.[17]

Telemedicine can help in initial patient onboarding, follow-up visits, and maintenance. Virtual primary care could likely serve single, healthy people under the age of forty all day long, whereas those who are married with kids and/or suffer from chronic ailments like high blood pressure, diabetes, or heart issues will still primarily go the route of personal visits.

Virtual primary care combined with medical-grade wearables and the Internet of Things could provide another technology infusion into healthcare.

Let's say your oxygen level drops from 98 to 94, your pulse increases from 67 to 80, and you have a low-grade fever.

Maybe you don't want to take a day off of work. You don't want to hassle your grandchildren to take you to the doctor. Instead of ignoring your symptoms, remote patient monitoring could lead to a quick telemedicine visit or even a text from your provider whose artificial intelligence is monitoring patients. Only then comes the decision on whether you take two aspirin and call your doctor in the morning or come into the office for a closer evaluation.

In a way, COVID-19, the mother of the mother of the mother of all Disruptions, could be just the opportunity that forces medical care to design better systems, accelerating healthcare into a future of better quality and lower prices.

In a real-life example, one medical device company executive I know suffered from occasional low oxygen levels that interrupted his sleep. His doctors, puzzled, issued him a remote medical monitoring device.

When business took my friend out of town, he did not follow his daily exercise regimen of swimming. His oxygen levels did not decline; his sleep was not interrupted.

Turns out, the businessman held his breath the length of every lap he swam, which reduced his blood oxygen level and woke him up at night.

The solution? Swim with a snorkel. Problem solved.

So it's already starting, where patients have a kit of devices that talk to each other and, more importantly, talk to their electronic medical record and give their doctor data, a kind of central alarm system for healthcare status.

Deploying wearables on ourselves, in our homes, and in our cars will yield a wealth of incredibly valuable data that will let our doctors know when something is out of kilter.

Artificial intelligence pouring through new waves of aggregated and consolidated data can yield new insights. Examining a 400,000-person cohort of patient volunteers, artificial intelligence could theoretically pinpoint that 137 patients who developed condition A showed changes in measurables X, Y, and Z. Monitoring those measurables before they reach the threshold that causes condition A could lead to future interventions that prevent health issues before they strike. In other words, wearable medical technology would help not only doctors and patients, but researchers as well.

Healthcare investors and insiders are adopting better business practices from other sectors and banking on technology and alternative Medicare models to provide better care, lower costs, and rewards to investors for innovation.

Investors and innovators with the foresight to deploy the right combination of technology, service, and innovation—the ones who can provide better patient outcomes at a lower cost —can use those insights to take advantage of Disruptions in healthcare. When those Disruptions lead to Tipping Points, they can ride those waves of Paradigm Shifts into profitable success.

Examples abound.

Carbon Health, a primary care provider, is tackling the burnout problem with a proprietary platform that eases the load on clinical staff. The startup aims to become the largest primary care provider in the U.S., delivering care across multiple channels: in-person, telemedicine, home-based virtual care, consumer health tools, and device-driven chronic disease management through apps. Within six years, it has doubled its staff, increased patient volume, and now operates more than 80 clinics in 12 states. Carbon Health has secured investments worth $552 million and has built a $3 billion-plus company.[18]

Curology is another startup using technology and innovation to target the supply-demand issue in dermatology, giving patients optionality.

Patients often wait months to make appointments with such specialists, which my wife Shari and I have experienced firsthand with our dermatologist.

When you finally get to the dermatologist (or any other medical provider), you wait a half hour before a nurse checks you in. Then, sometimes you wait another half hour before the doctor comes in. And if they need medical records from another provider, well, that can cost you weeks or months.

Third-party insurance, whether it's private like Humana or taxpayer-funded like Medicare, creates another layer of complexity. Bill paying is a nightmare. Shari spent five hours one day going between insurance and our dermatologist. As it turns out, our insurance company had been waiting months for documentation from our dermatologist to facilitate payment. Legions of consumers nationwide have similar stories.

The entire patient experience is terrible, offering opportunities to entrepreneurs who can navigate the waves of supply and demand, and the regulatory landscape. Their technology offers better service, medical record portability, better quality, and lower costs.

Curology cuts through a lot of the in-office medical red tape by using telemedicine to treat acne, delivering customized compounds to its patients. Starting out with pharmacies in San Diego and St. Louis, the company is expanding into Pittsburgh.

Acne, the most common skin condition in the United States, affects 85% of U.S. residents between the ages of 12 and 24, according to the American Academy of Dermatology.[19] For people in that age bracket, always glued to their cellphones, telemedicine fits perfectly with how they communicate.

Sure, you wouldn't want to use Curology if you suspected something serious, like skin cancer. But by taking some low-hanging fruit out of the system, such innovations can add capacity for more dire dermatological needs.

Other investors look to solve doctor burnout by heading to the acquisition table with private equity. Their goal is to buy primary care operations and implement technology and improved business practices, taking the administrative burden off the doctors.

Voilà —doctors can be doctors, physician assistants can be physician assistants, and nurses can be nurses. In primary care practices where medical personnel spend half their time on administration, such moves double medical capacity.

Walgreens is one player aiming to ride this wave, doubling down on what they call value-based primary care. The retail pharmacy has invested $5.2 billion in its partner VillageMD to co-locate one thousand pharmacies and full-service medical clinics inside its stores by 2027. The companies say they aim to significantly increase access to primary care in underserved communities.[20]

Other alternatives include opting out of the Medicare/third-party system in total.

Direct-to-patient care providers reckon that the entire system is in shambles, so why bother using it if you don't have to? Their foresight, if you will, is that governmental authorities and third-party insurers will never be able to reform such a tangled system, no matter how many laws, regulations, or armies of insurance adjusters surf into that maelstrom.

Direct-to-patient care providers charge consumers a flat $50-$100 monthly subscription fee, much less than a monthly insurance premium. The fee covers all in-office services, which can include electrocardiograms, biopsies, injections, splints for fractures, strep tests, urine tests, pregnancy tests, and more. Out-of-office lab tests can come at a 95% percent discount.[21]

When COVID-19 hit, direct-to-patient healthcare providers already offered 24/7 access to their clientele via telemedicine and phone consults. These doctors could immediately serve their patients at the lockdown's genesis without waiting for governments to relax regulations or for insurers to change reimbursement policies. A big advantage for direct-to-patient healthcare providers is that they didn't need to deal with a slew of new billing codes and bureaucratic changes.[22]

Direct primary care also benefits from not needing book-length reports from large consulting firms, years of study from the Centers for Medicare and Medicaid Services, large investments from outsiders, or rewrites of the books of laws and regulations that govern U.S. healthcare.

Whether the insights they and others have deployed can lead to Tipping Points that generate Paradigm Shifts toward more affordable, better-quality healthcare remains to be seen. But thanks to the Disruption of COVID-19, things are changing.

"There are generations where nothing happens," Roy Schoenberg, CEO of telemedicine company Amwell, told the healthcare news website Healthcare Dive. "There are decades where nothing happens. And there are weeks when decades happen. And that's exactly what we've gone through."[23]

These innovations pouring into healthcare can take advantage of the Disruptions of the last few years and perhaps sweep waves of change into a chaotic system to improve quality, decrease prices, and serve patients, clinicians, and investors.

Innovation combined with the Disruptions-Tipping Points-Paradigm Shifts playbook works in the automotive sector, robotics, material handling, and healthcare. It can work in whatever sector you specialize in as well.

We are indebted to Mike Futch, President and CEO of Tompkins Robotics, and Noel J. Guillama-Álvarez, Chairman of OXIO Health, for their gracious interviews about robotics/material handling and healthcare, respectively.

1. Klender, Joey. "Tesla Reveals Its Secret To Surviving Semiconductor Shortages." *Teslerati*, 26 Jul. 2021, www.teslarati.com/tesla-secret-surviving-semiconductor-shortage/.

2. "Tesla, Inc. (TSLA) Stock Historical Prices & Data." *Yahoo! Finance*, 21 Jun. 2022, finance.yahoo.com/quote/TSLA/history?period1=1551398400&period2=1558656000&interval=1d&filter=history&frequency=1d&includeAdjustedClose=true.

3. Stumpf, Rob. "At $631B, Tesla Is Now Worth More Than the Next Top 6 Car Companies Combined." TheDrive, 30 Dec. 2020, www.thedrive.

com/news/38485/at-631b-tesla-is-now-worth-more-than-the-next-top-6-car-companies-combined.

4. Furr, Nathan & Jeff Dyer. "Lessons from Tesla's Approach to Innovation." *Harvard Business Review*, 12 Feb. 2020, hbr.org/2020/02/lessons-from-teslas-approach-to-innovation.

5. Naik, Amit Raja. "All The Innovations By Tesla Beyond Electric Cars." *Analytics India Magazine*, 13 Jul. 2021, analyticsindiamag.com/all-the-innovations-by-tesla-beyond-electric-cars.

6. Shahan, Zachary. "A Short History of Tesla Critics' Claims." *CleanTechnica*, 4 Mar. 2019, cleantechnica.com/2019/03/04/a-short-history-of-tesla-critics-claims/.

7. "Tesla, Inc. (TSLA) Stock Historical Prices & Data." *Yahoo! Finance*, 21 Jun. 2022, finance.yahoo.com/quote/TSLA/history?period1=1551398400&period2=1558656000&interval=1d&filter=history&frequency=1d&includeAdjustedClose=true.

8. Futch, Mike. Personal Interview. 3 Dec. 2021.

9. Futch, Mike. Personal Interview. 3 Dec. 2021.

10. Futch, Mike. Personal Interview. 3 Dec. 2021.

11. Futch, Mike. Personal Interview. 3 Dec. 2021.

12. Futch, Mike. Personal Interview. 3 Dec. 2021.

13. Futch, Mike. Personal Interview. 3 Dec. 2021.

14. Guillama-Álvarez, Noel J. Personal Interview. 17 Nov. 2021.

15. "2020 Survey of America's Physicians COVID-19 Impact Edition." *Physicians Foundation*, Aug. 2020, physiciansfoundation.org/wp-content/uploads/2020/08/20-1278-Merritt-Hawkins-2020-Physicians-Foundation-Survey.6.pdf.

16. Guillama-Álvarez, Noel J. Personal Interview. 17 Nov. 2021.

17. Guillama-Álvarez, Noel J. Personal Interview. 17 Nov. 2021.

18. Landi, Heather. "Carbon Health Scoops Up Two Major Clinic Chains to Expand Primary Care Footprint." *Fierce Healthcare*, 24 Aug. 2021, www.fiercehealthcare.com/practices/carbon-health-scoops-up-two-major-clinic-chains-to-expand-primary-care-footprint.

19. "Skin Condition By The Numbers." *American Academy of Dermatology Association*, www.aad.org/media/stats-numbers.

20. "Walgreens Boots Alliance Makes $5.2 Billion Investment in VillageMD to Deliver Value-Based Primary Care to Communities Across America." *VillageMD*, 14 Oct. 2021, www.villagemd.com/press-releases/walgreens-boots-alliance-makes-5.2-billion-investment-in-villagemd-to-deliver-value-based-primary-care-to-communities-across-america.

21. Osterhoudt, John. "What Free Market Health Care Would Actually Look Like." *Reason Magazine*, Jul. 2021, reason.com/2021/06/19/what-free-market-health-care-would-actually-look-like/.

22. Bernard, Rebekah. "Direct Care Practices Perfectly Positioned to Help Patients During Coronavirus Outbreak." *Medical Economics*, 30 Mar. 2020, www.medicaleconomics.com/view/direct-care-practices-perfectly-positioned-help-patients-during-coronavirus-outbreak.

23. Pifer, Rebecca. "'Weeks Where Decades Happen': Telehealth 6 months into COVID-19." *Healthcare Dive*, 27 Jul. 2021, www.healthcaredive.com/news/telehealth-6-months-coronavirus/581447/.

12 INSTEAD OF FEARING OBSOLESCENCE, RIDE THE WAVE TO NEW SUCCESSES

Jeff Bezos has it right. No matter how long your enterprise lasts or how successful it is, you should be a startup every day. It's always Day 1, and you cannot be beholden to current paradigms. We must grasp that the old saying "success breeds success" is an obsolete paradigm. More often than not, success breeds failure, as the natural reality of organizations is to follow a cycle from startup to success to near obsolescence, repeating again. To stay on top—surfing the oceans of business from wave to wave to wave—Insightful Leaders must reinvent their organizations continually, not just every few years. With Disruption as the new normal, so, too, becomes reinvention.

"And once the storm is over, you won't remember how you made it through, how you managed to survive. You won't even be sure whether the storm is really over. But one thing is certain: When you come out of the storm, you won't be the same person who walked in. That's what this storm is all about."

FROM THE NOVEL *KAFKA ON THE SHORE* BY JAPANESE WRITER HARUKI MURAKAMI

Jeff Bezos has it right. Leaders who want to survive and thrive must treat every day as Day 1.

In his original 1997 letter to shareholders, the Amazon founder made the claim that "this is Day 1 for the Internet and, if we execute well, for Amazon.com."[1]

Bezos included the letter in every shareholder report, baking in Amazon's credo of thinking like a startup every day.[2] Bezos knew that no matter how powerful and accomplished his enterprise was, other innovators lurk. After all, his 1997 dispatch included nods to partnerships with now bought-out or bankrupt companies like America Online, Excite, Netscape, GeoCities, AltaVista, @Home, and Prodigy.

Unlike those long-gone entities, Bezos had the foresight to know that, instead of waiting to react to others, his enterprise could use the growing power of the internet to develop insights that would create Disruptions which would eventually create Tipping Points and Paradigm Shifts. By continually peering around corners and not resting on his successes, Bezos' brand of Insightful Leadership has allowed Amazon to surf from wave to wave to wave, never resting ashore—and never allowing their competitors to rest, either.

Instead of a circle of life (covered in Chapter 2) that leads to continual transformation and business success, most enterprises follow a standard path to near obsolescence. Startups begin in a valley, rise to the top, plateau, and then slowly decline. Chagrined, the board fires the old leadership team, bringing in fresh blood. If they're wise enough, the new leaders evaluate the corporation, create a vision, align the forces of the corporation behind that vision, pursue their goals, and win, and win, and win.

After singing hosannas and hallelujahs, leadership decides they must make sure no one screws this up, so they put rules and procedures in place to maintain their top positions, all while forgetting how they got there in the first place.

These solid but non-Insightful Leaders think they are resting on the mountaintop. They wake up one morning and feel their hair blowing. They wonder why and look around.

Turns out, they weren't on a mountain; their organization was on the crest of a wave in the middle of the ocean, far away from any hilltops. Now, instead of reinventing, they're sliding down from the wave's crest into a trough, ready to be swallowed up by the sea of Disruption.

While the leaders were busy protecting their vision, that vision became obsolete. They lose market share and get fired.

And the cycle restarts, because in a world where Disruption is the new normal, there is no solid ground nor dry land, only the turbulent waters of the ocean.

Perhaps new leadership will have the enterprise cresting on top of the waves again. But then, instead of reinventing, they will get content, remain satisfied, resist change, protect what they have done and, when the current waves break, get swallowed by the surf.

Insightful Leaders, instead, continually operate as startups. The circle of life from Chapter 2 tells us we must reinvent to be successful. Reinvention in a world where Disruption is the new normal requires following the process of Insightful Leadership outlined in Chapter 1, a process of continually gaining insights, harnessing the power of insights, and creating success.

The Innovation Cycle (Figure 12.1) is a more detailed view of the Insightful Leadership process. In fact, the Innovation Cycle is the process of reinvention from the circle of life in much more detail. Moving your enterprise from the left side of the Innovation Cycle (where the circle of life becomes the circle of death) to the right side—and keeping it there—is the only way to avoid wiping out in a world of perpetual Disruption.

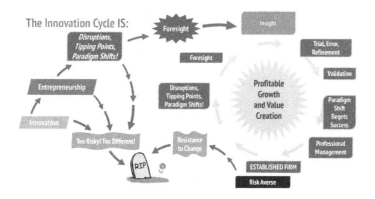

Figure 12.1

The Innovation Cycle

As author Haruki Murakami states, you—and your enterprise —won't be the same as when you walked into the storm, just as Amazon is a much different (and much larger and more powerful) company than it was in 1997.

Murakami writes that you won't be sure whether the storm is over. In a world of COVID-19, digital innovation, geopolitical/financial crises, broken supply chains, inflation, wars, and potential wars, that question is no longer valid, as the storm never will retreat.

That's why the Innovation Cycle, like Disruption, is perpetual. In other words, on Day 3, Amazon was not the same company it was on Day 1, but it was back to Day 1 again.

As with many things in business, the Innovation Cycle begins with, of course, innovation, as seen in the bottom left corner of Figure 12.1.

This innovation can flow to entrepreneurship, where leadership can move forward or assign labels to it like "too risky," "too expensive," "bad timing," or "too different." Labeling leads to the graveyard, as such innovations never see daylight. These aren't moonshots that fail to reach the lunar surface or rockets that go off course, but ideas that never receive enough energy or backing to clear the launch pad. These entrepreneurs never even get on their surfboards.

This is the way to obsolescence: giving your enterprise no chance to ride the wave to future successes.

If entrepreneurs have the foresight to greenlight these innovations and pair them with the correct insights, these innovations could point the way forward toward competitive advantage, becoming a Disruption, Tipping Point, and Paradigm in and of themselves.

To make sure your leadership team has a robust understanding of what foresights and insights need to be gained, you must ask five questions coming out of the entrepreneurship box of the Innovation Cycle:

1. What impacts do Disruptions, Tipping Points, and Paradigm Shifts have on our supply chains?
2. What impacts do Disruptions, Tipping Points, and Paradigm Shifts have on our competitors' supply chains?
3. If this innovation we created can turn into a Disruption, Tipping Point, and Paradigm Shift, what are its impacts?
4. What impacts will this new Disruption, Tipping Point, and Paradigm Shift have on our industry?
5. What impact will this new Disruption, Tipping

Point, and Paradigm Shift have on the global
geopolitical and business community?

The answers to these questions help generate foresight, or
knowing what Tipping Points and Paradigm Shifts will come
from Disruptions. Based on these foresights, Insightful
Leaders can gain insights into their businesses, their
customers, the competition, and the future trends that will
shape the competitive landscape.

Insight, on the other hand, results from lateral thinking
about what will happen from Disruptions, Tipping Points,
and Paradigm Shifts. This creative, indirect approach uses
intuition and imagination in an unstructured way.

Contrast this with the vertical thinking necessary for foresight. Vertical thinking is the analytical process of going
through a set of sequential steps, much like the traditional
engineering approach to solving problems:

- Define the problem.
- Analyze the problem.
- Generate alternative solutions.
- Evaluate alternative solutions.
- Select the best solution.
- Implement the solution.

Lateral thinking is what you see in artists or philosophers.
Vertical thinking is what you see in engineers or computer
scientists. Insightful Leaders must have a foot in both worlds.
It's no coincidence that two of the most celebrated biogra-
phies of the last decades (both penned by Walter Isaacson)
were *Steve Jobs* and *Leonardo da Vinci*.

As you can see around the top of the right-hand circle in
Figure 12.1, foresights and insights are the raw fuel that
Insightful Leaders use to develop the action plans necessary
for the organization to harness the power of their insights and,

hence, the power of Disruptions, Tipping Points, and Paradigm Shifts.

Now Not Serving Customer XYZ

A word of caution, however, about those action plans. Remember that Disruption is the new normal; therefore, your action plans must be adaptive enough to flex with future Disruptions, Tipping Points, and Paradigm Shifts. Focused, adaptable action plans based on correct insights will attract and retain customers, achieving an exceptional return for all stakeholders.

Foresight must answer the question: "Based on our insights, where are we going?" To define the *where*, we first need to answer the *who*, *what*, and *how*.

Who are the customers you will serve? Customer segmentation slices many ways—B2B, B2C, and now B2ME, obviously, but which B2B, B2C, and B2ME? Are you targeting huge, global conglomerates or small, regional customers? Do your customers want inexpensive or premium products? Once we get specific on target customers to serve, we need to get specific on their expectations, desires, and requirements.

A key portion of defining *who* to serve is deciding who *not* to serve. This can be done with a traditional industrial engineering process of A-B-C segmentation.

For example, the president of one Northeast U.S. electronics distributor I worked with was frustrated because his sales force spent a large share of its time on activities that yielded no profit. Instead of the 80-20 or Pareto rule (pay keen attention to the 20% of your customers who generate 80% of your profit), they were paying attention to the squeaky wheel, missing the core of how they generated profits.

My analysis confirmed his assumptions.

Like the Pareto rule states, 20% of this company's customers resulted in 80% of the profit, 40% of the customers generated 20% of the profit, and the other 40% returned zero profits.

Many in the zero-profit group were in development-type conditions. They would order semiconductor number 123, semiconductor number 456, and semiconductor number 789. Therefore, distribution opened three packs with one hundred semiconductors each to pick out, repack, and deliver three semiconductors. Customers selected the correct semiconductor for development, returned the other two, and often never contacted the electronics distributorship again.

Beyond the excess labor, repackaging, and shelving problems, sales staffers would spend up to fifteen hours a week with such customers, accomplishing no sales of any significance. In fact, with the cost of returns, the eighty cent profit on one semiconductor quickly turned into lost money.

This company president, although appreciative of my analysis, didn't like the terms A-B-C or even red-green-yellow for segmentation. Both placed negative connotations on the lower-tiered customers.

After consultation, we came up with blue, green, and orange. Blue customers were long-term clients who placed at least two orders a month and generated at least $200,000 a year in business. Businesses want to do everything possible to make sure these customers are happy. You take them to lunch, send them tickets to the ballgame or theater, and spend time with them.

Green clients, while having much potential, resulted in no substantial profit. Remember, they were 40% of the customer base but only 20% of the profit. And some weren't even holding their own. So we established a series of rules that forced them to become profitable and pay their own way, which made a lot of sense. Orders less than $50 were charged a $50 processing fee. Those small orders cost the distributor $22 to invoice and collect, and the electronic product that yields $22 of margin on a $50 order is rare indeed. This encouraged green clients to decide on larger, more profitable orders.

Orange customers were relegated to online ordering. No questions, research, or returns were available. Payment was up front, eliminating invoicing costs, and shipping costs were assigned at the time of the order.

Staff went through their customers and put orange labels on their file tabs and wherever their names appeared in the electronic distributorship's system. If an orange customer sent sales an order, sales simply did not respond.

That's not very friendly, right? Well, that was the president's objective—these customers could no longer drown large percentages of his sales team's time into a vortex below the waves of profitability.

Results were stellar. The blue customer base grew about 10%, the green customer base grew about 30%, and the unimportant orange customer base went down by about 40%.

Fewer customers. More profit.

Many companies say they want to sell to anyone and everyone, but if you're in Fargo, North Dakota, do you really want to serve Perth, Australia? Does that make sense for your supply chain? Should you not define what geographical boundaries you serve? If you plan to offer premium service, you must have a customer base willing to pay for premium.

Your action plan must really, really, really understand who you're selling to and what deals to make with those people.

That can make the difference between making money and obsolescence.

Even in "normal" times, not every customer is worth having. Now that inflation is back on the radar for the first time since 1982, that notion is even more important. Chasing market share for the sake of market share runs the risk of basking in inflationary revenue, not real revenue. Cash flow will become even more important, so enterprises should concentrate on the market segments that are more profitable and let the others go. Cash-inefficient customers can be killers.[3]

Such decisions on who and what segments to serve depend on where you are in the market.

Nordstrom understands its customer base very well, touting its customer service to the world.

One story tells of a Nordstrom customer preparing for a sales presentation in Japan. He realized he only packed one business shoe. He could wear sneakers to the corporate meeting room, go barefoot, or wear one sneaker and one dress shoe—not wise options.

This long-standing customer called his personal shopper. The personal shopper realized the customer had purchased wingtip dress shoes at the Nordstrom Perimeter Mall in Metro Atlanta six weeks ago. The personal shopper overnights a new pair in that style, delivering them into the shopper's hands as he is waiting in the lobby for his meeting.

The salesman gave a successful presentation in a matching pair of dress shoes and won the order.

Fantastic service.

Fantastic cost, as well.

While I might not want to set those kinds of expectations, Nordstrom's customers expect it. That's one reason why Nordstrom charges higher prices than Walmart.

The Paradigm Shift of B2ME

Differing customer expectations are also a harbinger of the world of Disruptions-Tipping Points-Paradigm Shifts brought on by COVID-19, digital innovation, geopolitical/financial crises, and their longstanding, cumulative effects.

As I noted in Chapter 8, customers have switched beyond the traditional B2B and B2C to B2ME. Traditional B2B has Staples shipping four orders a month to Big Conglomerate headquarters. But with office workers dispersed to homes, Big Conglomerate now places dozens of orders a month, and instead of heading to HQ, those orders go to this man's home, this woman's home, this other guy's home, and so on.

This new paradigm skyrockets delivery costs, but Staples still calls that B2B because the definition of B2B is when products or services are sold from one business to another. Well, B2B implies that deliveries go to businesses, but the work-from-home Paradigm Shift has changed that to B2ME.

Today, there are more one-box B2ME shipments like Nordstrom's delivery to its customer in Japan, not a pallet of office supplies from Staples. Although costs will go up when sending out one-box shipments, try not to approach the Nordstrom level of service costs.

The point is, the work-from-home Tipping Point has changed who your customers are and what they want.

This will often change your unique selling proposition for these customers. Your unique selling proposition succinctly outlines how your business, product, or service differs from your competition. It identifies what makes your business the better choice and why your target clients should choose you over the competition.

Uncovering your unique selling proposition requires putting yourself in your customer's shoes. Too often, companies fall in love with their product or service. You must remember that companies exist to satisfy their customers' needs, not their own. Step back from your daily operations and scrutinize what your customers really want.

Simultaneously, you must ensure that your unique selling proposition provides your stakeholders a great outcome. Often, a company must go back and assess its *who*, because when it got to its *what*, it realized that customer needs were inconsistent with the enterprise's ability to succeed. Customer needs must be defined in the context of the company's needs, including customers, the end-to-end supply chain, employees, stockholders, and the community at large.

Now that you have answered the *who* and the *what*, you

need to answer the *how*. A clear action plan will define what innovations you will pursue to achieve your foresight.

I had the good fortune to meet Major League Baseball Hall of Fame catcher Yogi Berra once during a Dodgers-Yankees World Series. I asked him why the Dodgers were winning.

In typical Yogi fashion, the Yankees' legend retorted, "They are scoring more runs than we are."

He was right, but his observation had little to do with how the Yankees could beat the Dodgers. At a high level, such optional action plans would include deploying strategies that minimized the runs scored by the Dodgers and/or deploying strategies that put more runs on the board for the Yankees.

Of course, multiple innovations could achieve these two high-level action plans—more powerful hitting, more stolen bases, better pitching, defensive shifts, etc.

Leadership must put forth achievable innovations that will result in the greatest benefit to customers, your end-to-end supply chain, your employees, your stockholders, and your community.

Walmart is an excellent example of an enterprise that has repeatedly developed action plans to help the enterprise travel around the Innovation Cycle.

Even before COVID-19, the mega-retailer's Insightful Leadership had the foresight to gauge how digital innovation was affecting their markets. No, they didn't foresee a global pandemic Disruption skyrocketing online sales during 2020, but they anticipated that the eCommerce Tipping Point would result in a Paradigm Shift at some point in the future.

So, Walmart's insight was to invest heavily in eCommerce, even before the pandemic struck.[4] That move gave its systems options. Those options allowed Walmart customers to park their cars and click on their keyboards to shop during COVID-19 outbreaks.

While many analysts have predicted the demise of physical stores, Walmart has used optionality to prove that retail stores can be an asset, not an albatross, in the eCommerce world.

It turns out that many shoppers—even those who make purchases online—like having a store to visit for customer service and returns. Such activities are possible in Walmart's more than five thousand U.S. stores, whereas Amazon only has around six hundred U.S. stores (most of them are Whole Foods). Walmart's status as the largest grocer in the U.S. also helps, as does its decision to expand curbside pickup on its grocery app to include non-grocery items.[5]

Walmart also has mimicked Amazon's Prime membership with its own Walmart+, which the giant retailer has been heavily promoting. Walmart+ membership includes free shipping from Walmart.com, free shipping from your nearby store, discounts on prescriptions and fuel, and the ability to check out with your phone while you shop in the store. Their advertisements claim more benefits are being added.[6]

Walmart's action plan allows its online retail revenue to grow five times faster than Amazon's, with a 74% increase in eCommerce sales in the first quarter of 2021.[7]

Even Action Has Its Limits

To travel from wave to wave to wave, it is wise to limit such action plans to five or six items. One or two of them could help the enterprise continuously move to the next wave, another one or two could make small steps toward the wave *after* the next wave, and the last one or two should be big steps toward that third wave. If we don't want to feel the wind in our hair as our surfboard tumbles into the trough (not to mention soaking our hair!), we must always prepare for waves beyond the one we are striving toward.

Traditionally, deployment of action plans was straightforward: "Just get it done!"

This neglected the fact that, to have a chance to remain on the right-hand side of the Innovation Cycle, each action plan must include trial, error, and refinement for validation. Pursuing action plans without trial, error, and refinement often begets brittle solutions which, at the slightest disturbance, perform as well as a surfboard in a typhoon. While this might have worked for a while in a stable environment, this is sometimes unhelpful when Disruption is the new normal. Such plans do not have the adaptability to provide the success inherent to the innovation.

Brittle action plans are not necessarily wrong. They just do not reflect the reality of today's environment. Trial, error, and refinement are critical for our innovation-foresight-insight to meet or exceed expectations. Strictly adhering to action plans, an asset in stable times, is an absolute curse in turbulent times.

I have made some boneheaded mistakes. I would not eliminate those mistakes, for they have made me who I am. In fact, I won't call them mistakes; I'll call them "learning by fire." Fire teaches great lessons.

Similarly, having an open mind to learning while pursuing action plans is more important than following said plan's "letter of the law." Unless mistakes are of the intentional variety that destroy integrity or respect, mistakes/learning by fire should result in lessons learned, not employees terminated.

A culture of trial and error is an organizational strength in turbulent times.

Alignment When Everything Changes

Now that we have solid, refined, and validated action plans, we can move to the next hurdle: alignment, making sure that all employees work together toward the same goal.

The replacement of visionary leadership with Insightful Leadership does not, unfortunately, negate this difficult step. The path is lit by the Innovation Cycle, while Disruptions-Tipping Points-Paradigm Shifts, foresights, insights, and action plans act as guiding beacons for organizations that successfully deploy innovation after innovation. Broken paths, however, could serve as reminders of the organization's hypocrisy, past failed attempts to bring about change.

Organizations that travel from wave to wave versus those that travel from wave to wipeout differ in two ways: 1) the quality of their path, and 2) the quality of their alignment with their path.

In today's turbulent times, no one is autonomous. All organizational connections and all employees are interdependent. A focused group working together and pulling in the same direction acts as a powerful single unit, pursuing action plans, succeeding, improving performance, and generating a sense of unity and accomplishment. Organizations with disparate elements that pull in different directions, on the other hand, bring about demoralization, failure, and a sense of futility.

The necessity of continual change makes alignment even more difficult than in previous eras. Without clarity from Insightful Leaders, your workforce could see targeting multiple waves as evidence that you lack a firm focus. You must communicate that the times we are in, not C-suite irresolution, are creating the need for ongoing reinvention. This will require a solid communication plan and open doors to managers and employees at all levels.

In an age where Disruption is the new normal, you are asking your organization to align with a new set of action plans targeting the next wave while your employees are still completing the last set of action plans, all while keeping in mind the third wave on the distant horizon. The default for humans is resistance to change; it is only natural for a group that has climbed Mount Kilimanjaro to want a break before tackling Mount Everest. Traveling wave to wave to wave requires that your workforce tackle Mount Kilimanjaro and Mount Everest at the same time, all while throwing the Matterhorn in between.

However, the benefits can be tremendous.

Take Walmart's heavy eCommerce investment noted above. As the mega-retailer travels along the wave of eCommerce, that investment has opened up a new business: selling its buy-online-pick-up-in-store technology to mid- and small-sized retailers. Those retailers can then add products to Walmart's online marketplace, similar to Amazon's—another Innovation Cycle for Walmart to travel.[8]

You can liken enterprises like Walmart to the surfer who brings multiple surfboards to the beach. When the waves change in intensity, optionality allows them to switch boards and keep surfing the waves of Disruption.

Your workforce must understand that this is the new normal. One innovation every five years is not sufficient for success when facing never-ending Disruptions-Tipping Points-Paradigm Shifts.

The Importance of Culture and Professional Management

For Insightful Leaders to align their organizations to the Innovation Cycle, it is crucial to understand and address culture and professional management.

Culture can be hard to define, is often unseen, and is intangible. But culture results from the synthesis of rules, habits, procedures, standards, norms, rewards, language, jargon, stories, expectations, and ceremonies that go into how an organization chooses its employees and how those employees conform to those discrete manifestations.

That behavior, or culture, determines how your employees act under pressure, how they deal with customers, how they interact with each other, how they make decisions, and, ultimately, whether they accept and contribute to action plans.

The simplest way to put it is this: culture is how your workforce thinks your organization works. A simple statement of "we don't do that like this" is a manifestation of culture.

Whether your personnel take that statement as an end to conversation or a reason to ask "perhaps we should" can define whether your culture is amenable to the change necessary in a world of Disruptions-Tipping Points-Paradigm Shifts or whether personnel will cling to the existing operational reality.

Culture permeates all organizational activities and events and plays an important role in moving organizations from wave to wave.

While culture can be difficult to see, its manifestations are tangible, visible, and often well-defined. Cultural manifestations include:

- Office apparel
- Working remotely versus working from the office
- Executive perks
- Seating arrangements
- Organizational stories, jargon, ceremonies, titles, etc.
- Work-life balance

An organization's culture is initially created in the minds of its founders. As organizations evolve, so do their cultures. Cultural transformation is difficult because it requires transforming rules, habits, procedures, standards, norms, rewards, language, jargon, stories, expectations, ceremonies, and titles. However, cultural transformation is necessary to change an organization from one that seeks small, incremental improvements to one that deploys repeated innovations in response to Disruptions-Tipping Points-Paradigm Shifts. Leaders understand that existing cultures always fight to maintain the status quo. Therefore, to reinvent the organization, the leader must first reinvent the culture.

The best way to grasp the culture necessary to travel wave to wave is to understand what Jeff Bezos means by Day 1. Bezos sees Day 1 as a day of risk-accepting mentality, which fosters innovation, speed, and nimbleness. Unfortunately, as many organizations grow in size and complexity, layers and rules creep in. The organization slows, becoming more rigid and risk-averse. To Bezos, Day 1 means that even though Amazon will aggressively grow in size and scope, it will retain the entrepreneurial vitality and nimbleness of a startup.

This contrasts with Bezos' vision of Day 2, where many enterprises reside. Day 2 includes:

- Stagnation
- Wave to wipeout
- Irrelevance
- Decline
- Death

In a way, Bezos does not need the foresight portion of the Innovation Cycle. Instead of anticipating which Tipping Points and Paradigm Shifts will come from Disruptions, Bezos creates the Disruptions that lead to Tipping Points and Paradigm Shifts, forcing other enterprises to keep up. The digital innovation that allowed eCommerce to reach a Tipping Point was in place before the COVID-19 Disruption, and that innovation largely came from Amazon and other tech titans.

With Disruption as the new normal, Day 1 becomes more important than ever as the endless cycle of Disruptions-Tipping Points-Paradigm Shifts requires that we continuously innovate from one wave to the next, to the next, to the next.

This brings us to the double-edged sword known as professional management, although in our case, this is perhaps more like a dual-use surfboard designed to handle both small waves and large ones.

Professional management, despite its tendency toward lethargy, is necessary to implement the action plans needed to transform your organization into an adaptive enterprise.

Adaptive enterprises embrace the optionality required to respond to Disruptions-Tipping Points-Paradigm Shifts.

Adaptive enterprises are the opposite of brittle organizations that limit their ambitions to optimality.

Your organization requires leadership to engage professional management to assure the organization is ready to travel wave to wave to wave. Professional management's role is to ensure the organization adapts to this ongoing reinvention.

Professional management must answer four questions to make sure the organization evolves to keep up with continuous reinvention:

1. Structure: Do we have the organizational structure that supports our wave-to-wave journey? Do we have the correct roles, responsibilities, and processes for the journey to the next wave?
2. People: Do we have the right people in the right roles? Do they understand the importance of being an adaptive enterprise? Are the people aligned with our innovations and action plans? Are they capable of implementing the action plans? Are they correctly incentivized and motivated to succeed?
3. Culture: Are rules, behaviors, procedures, norms, expectations, etc. driving growth, vision, learning, quick decision-making, and wave-to-wave performance?
4. Measures: Are we measuring the right key performance indicators? Are there factors which have resulted from our innovations and action plans that suggest we change what we measure?

As professional management, under the guidance of Insightful Leadership, leads to more innovation and success, your enterprise faces an important question: are we satisfied with navigating the waves of Disruptions-Tipping Points-Paradigm Shifts, or do we want to become the force behind future Disruptions-Tipping Points-Paradigm Shifts?

This is the downside of professional management—the tendency to rest on our laurels or travel solely on inertia.

Again, the tendency is normal. You have succeeded. Stakeholders are blissful. Customers are satisfied.

Aversion to risk is natural. Risk implies danger, jeopardy, peril, hazard, and menace—not something your average employee courts, much less your professional management. But the more risk-averse the organization, the more the people bathe in their success, resist change, and fail to understand that the wind blowing through their hair comes because they are tumbling from their surfboard, not traveling to the next wave.

If your organization reaches the "established firm" box on the Innovation Cycle, do not succumb to the broken path to the left. The resistance to change box in Figure 12.1 leads to the graveyard. In the new world of Disruptions-Tipping Points-Paradigm Shifts, resistance to change is not just futile; it is death.

The true path to success is the yellow brick road (or, more accurately in the case of Figure 12.1, the line of arrows), which leads back to more Disruptions-Tipping Points-Paradigm Shifts. The cycle immediately repeats.

While surfers normally take breaks between waves, your organization cannot.

Instead, implementing action plans requires leadership to convert the negativity surrounding resistance to change into a positive force that supports nonstop wave-to-wave reinvention.

This is a major leadership challenge. Your teams have done a fantastic job, and their excitement for the latest innovation is still growing, so it's understandable that they would have a difficult time moving on to the next action plan.

This is why the Insightful Leaders of adaptive organizations must not dwell on moving from the current state to a future state—from wave to wave. Insightful Leaders will push the ongoing process of moving (or perhaps moooooooooooving) from wave to wave to wave.

The only way to accomplish this effectively, without resistance to change, is for your workforce to understand that Disruption is the new normal. Either embrace turbulence and continue to travel around the Innovation Cycle, or be risk averse, resist change, and accept that your organization will fail.

This is where communication is key. Leadership must:

1. fully communicate the Innovation Cycle,
2. fully communicate current Disruptions-Tipping Points-Paradigm Shifts, foresights, insights, and action plans,
3. fully communicate successes and actively recognize participation,
4. identify and eliminate any obstacles to the successful deployment of innovations and action plans
5. and celebrate success, demonstrate determination, and exhibit confidence.

You can surf the waves of a turbulent world or wipe out. The choice is up to you and your organization.

---

1. Bezos, Jeff. "To Our Shareholders." 1997, s2.q4cdn.com/299287126/files/doc_financials/annual/Shareholderletter97.pdf.
2. Slater, Daniel. "Elements of Amazon's Day 1 Culture." *AWS Executive Insights*, 2021, aws.amazon.com/executive-insights/content/how-amazon-defines-and-operationalizes-a-day-1-culture/.
3. Charan, Ram. "Leading Through Inflation: What The CEO Must Do." *Chief Executive Group*, 1 Mar. 2022, chiefexecutive.net/leading-through-inflation-what-the-ceo-must-do/.
4. Reagan, Courtney. "Walmart's Latest Business: Selling its E-commerce Tech to Other Retailers." *CNBC*, 28 Jul. 2021, www.cnbc.com/2021/07/28/walmart-to-sell-e-commerce-technology-to-smaller-retailers-.html.

5. Kestenbaum, Richard. "Walmart Is Gaining On Amazon In E-Commerce." *Forbes*, 20 Oct. 2021, www.forbes.com/sites/richardkestenbaum/2021/10/20/walmart-is-gaining-on-amazon-in-e-commerce/?sh=45f24b24653c.

6. "Free 30-Day Trial." *Walmart*, www.walmart.com/plus.

7. Segal, Edward. "How Walmart Is Responding To Covid-Related Challenges." *Forbes*, 1 Sep. 2021, www.forbes.com/sites/edwardsegal/2021/09/01/how-covid-repeatedly-put-walmart-to-the-test/?sh=1574713417bd.

8. Reagan, Courtney. "Walmart's Latest Business: Selling its E-commerce Tech to Other Retailers." *CNBC*, 28 Jul. 2021, www.cnbc.com/2021/07/28/walmart-to-sell-e-commerce-technology-to-smaller-retailers-.html.

13 SURF'S UP. WILL YOUR ENTERPRISE FLOUNDER OR RIDE ON?

From now on, whatever new normal you figure out will soon be swept away by the waves of the future. Optimally solving problems won't work. Instead, business leaders must have the foresight to position their enterprises to catch the waves (Disruptions), navigate those waves when they break (Tipping Points), use their insight to assess how the waves will advance (Paradigm Shifts), and harness the power of those waves to ride into the future (innovations). Leadership is no longer about having a vision and aligning your enterprise's operations with that vision. Instead, Insightful Leadership for today and the future is about looking around the corner and taking the steps necessary to allow us to get ahead of the competition and create competitive advantage. The greatest opportunity for innovation comes now when history is accelerated. This will be achieved by embracing Insightful Leadership and riding from wave to wave and more.

Historically, managers and leaders have planned to stifle Disruption. Consistency was the name of the game. With Disruption as the new normal—particularly during inflationary times—that planning leads to mirages, not solutions. Consistency is gone. It is not the era we operate in.

But remember, not all Disruptions are created equal. Some will go away, some will create new norms, and some will create avalanches of new normals. For example, a hurricane destroying a hundred houses in Wilmington, N.C. is certainly dire, but presuming there's no loss of life, the houses will be rebuilt and life will return to normal for most people.

The destruction caused by COVID-19, on the other hand, has created a series of tsunamis, abetted by the digital innovations of the 21st century and geopolitical/financial crises. The three big Tipping Points of lockdowns, eCommerce, and broken supply chains will continue evolving and creating more Disruptions, hence my argument that Disruption is the new normal and that leaders, instead of climbing a mountaintop to rest at the peak of their success, must surf wave to wave, never resting ashore.

How do you differentiate typical Disruptions from the bigger, Black Swan type? Let's revisit my process from Chapter 1, a series of thought experiments I have used for years but only recently formalized for the era of Insightful Leadership. This is the process that has repeatedly kept my organizations operating in the right-hand circle of the Innovation Cycle, Figure 12.1 from Chapter 12.

1. Gaining insights
2. Harnessing the power of insights
3. Creating success from Insightful Leadership

1. Gaining Insights

Remember the two pillars of Insightful Leadership: peering around corners and surfing the waves of our turbulent world.

The best question any entrepreneur or leader can ask is this: "How do you establish insight?" The best answer is this: "Peering around corners."

This is your environmental scan: knowing your market, knowing what's happening, researching and learning even beyond your comfort zone, and asking yourself, "What is going to result in my business changing?"

Again, my three steps for gaining insights are:

1. Scanning your environment: identifying Disruptions and understanding their impacts; peering around corners.
2. Developing insights: by studying Disruptions, anticipate Tipping Points and envision Paradigm Shifts.
3. Documenting insights: specify shifts in the future of business that provide opportunities for competitive advantage.

For example, I was looking at the growth of eCommerce early in this millennium when eCommerce totaled around 2% of all retail sales. But it was growing—2.5%, 3%, all the way to 7.2% by 2015.[1] Small numbers to start with, but the eCommerce wave rode on.

This gave me the foresight to know that the eCommerce wave would hit a Tipping Point and accelerate. My guess was that it would happen around 2025. I, like many others, didn't expect a worldwide pandemic to accelerate history in early 2020.

Used to be, fulfillment services offered you two delivery options: fast and expensive or slow and cheap. But the market was moving toward demanding fast and cheap, which cannot be handled with a warehouse or two out in the middle of nowhere, where land is cheap but distance to customers is long.

The analysis of these market trends serves as the perfect

example of developing insight by studying Disruptions. Documenting that insight and specifying the shifts in the future of business led to Distributed Logistics—companies were going to need smaller warehouses positioned closer to their customers, at least eight or so for nationwide service.

The environmental scans helped me peer around corners and see what was likely to happen (again, anticipating, not forecasting the future—after all, my forecast was off by five years!). I developed insight by reviewing the Disruptions coming from eCommerce, anticipating the Tipping Points, and watching the marketplace shift from being okay with getting a package in a few days to demanding order fulfillment within a day or two.

Walmart, Kohl's, and other giant retailers have been constructing Distributed Logistics systems for several years. The kings, of course, are Amazon and Jeff Bezos. Amazon operates more than one thousand delivery centers of some sort or another nationwide.[2]

While you might aspire to build such a system, your drivers should be customer service and volume, not to become bigger or smaller.

In other words, if your sector involves producing and shipping goods to customers who want two-day delivery, your organization needs fulfillment capabilities in five locations. Example locations could include Allentown, Pennsylvania; Atlanta, Georgia; Dallas, Texas; Chicago, Illinois; and Reno, Nevada. If you only have the volume and resources to justify having two fulfillment centers, the other three locations need to be solid third-party logistics providers (3PLs).

If, however, your customers desire next-day delivery, you need eight to ten sites with fulfillment capabilities, perhaps adding Los Angeles and San Francisco in California; Memphis, Tennessee; Salt Lake City, Utah; and Columbus, Ohio.

That number jumps to eighteen to twenty-four sites for

same-day delivery. Such a Distributed Logistics network could include:

- Los Angeles, California
- San Francisco, California
- Salt Lake City, Utah
- Seattle, Washington
- Phoenix, Arizona
- Denver, Colorado
- Dallas, Texas
- Houston, Texas
- Kansas City, Kansas
- Memphis, Tennessee
- Raleigh, North Carolina
- Atlanta, Georgia
- Port St. Lucie, Florida
- Minneapolis, Minnesota
- Chicago, Illinois
- Columbus, Ohio
- Louisville, Kentucky
- Pittsburgh, Pennsylvania
- Allentown, Pennsylvania
- Boston, Massachusetts

Your level of desired customer service is directly proportional to the number of fulfillment centers and shipment hubs.

That's a major Paradigm Shift in the logistics business. Most companies cannot build and operate eight, ten, or twenty-four fulfillment and distribution centers. That's why I created, built, and sold a Distributed Logistics business even before the waves of COVID-19 washed ashore.

This is how, as an "established firm" on the bottom right-hand side of the Innovation Cycle (Figure 12.1), you navigate through the Disruptions-Tipping Points-Paradigm Shifts to create new insights to continually surf the waves to success. If you take that left-hand turn on the bottom of the Innovation Cycle, falling into the box marked "resistance to change," you surf right into the graveyard.

But taking that right-hand turn toward more Disruptions, Tipping Points, and Paradigm Shifts is what you must do. Your thinking must be ahead of the market, and you have to anticipate what's going to happen.

Another way to express this is to bewail the corporate evil that is strategic planning and budgeting. Planners assume the future is going to be like the past, which is to say paradigms will not shift, so they add 2% for increased revenue and this cost and that cost and that forecast and project the future. That certainly did not work in 2021, when inflation alone shot costs up 7%,[3] and it will not work in the future. If you're an established company, you know the drill; if you're a budding entrepreneur, please avoid this!

This assumes the past is a good indicator of the future. In a world where Disruption is the new normal, the past is not a good indicator of the future. Paradigms will shift.

Instead of so-called strategic planning, you must think deeply about what other things are going to happen and how you envision them playing out.

Most of today's managers and executives concern themselves with what's happening now and how it will progress. Insightful Leaders, on the other hand, do not just look at today. Our environmental scanning helps us peer around corners so we can develop insights—what is going to change, what is going to alter the industry—and document those insights into specific shifts in the future of business to get ahead of the competition.

Let's take inflation, for example, a phenomenon that business executives and entrepreneurs have not concerned themselves with for two generations. If your distribution system expands from offering two-day delivery to next-day delivery, will that generate enough cash flow in real (not inflated) dollars to justify the expense? On the other hand, can you afford not to expand now, when interest rates for property acquisition remain at historically low levels?

Well, if you have integrated Digital Supply Networks into your operations, you are primed to adapt as others flounder. Enterprises that could rely on real-time data and analytics prospered during COVID-19,[4] and they will be able to replicate that success in the future, reacting to market changes before their competition. Digital Supply Networks will drive inefficiencies and costs out of your enterprise's end-to-end supply chain, keeping the costs of goods sold low. Your increases in price, likely made necessary if inflation continues at a 6-8% clip, will be less steep and less shocking to your customers' sensibilities and bottom line.

Indeed, Digital Supply Networks could help your enterprise embrace the Disruption of inflation, surfing through that Tipping Point and remaining relevant if the Paradigm Shift takes business back to the inflationary 1970s.

2. Harnessing the Power of Insights

Of course, developing insights without the ability to harness them is about as useful as bringing a shortboard to the beach to handle twenty-foot-plus waves.

To harness the power of insights and navigate today's turbulent business world, Insightful Leaders must:

1. Define obsolete paradigms: identify specific paradigms which, due to Disruptions and Tipping Points, are no longer correct.
2. Develop a strategy to replace obsolete paradigms: identify innovations that will replace obsolete paradigms.

For the new eCommerce era of Distributed Logistics, the first step was defining the obsolete paradigm: large fulfillment facilities in the middle of nowhere on cheap land. The next step was developing the strategy and innovation necessary to replace it: smaller fulfillment centers closer to customers for speedier delivery.

My Insightful Leadership process works in every sector, even those I'm not especially well-versed in, like gasoline production versus electric vehicles.

Recently, there's been a large movement to prevent the development of gasoline pipelines. If we cannot get gasoline through pipelines, though, won't this effectively hold us hostage? What will happen to gasoline prices? You can look at the news and answer that one for yourself.

Of course, we can all move to electric vehicles, but virtually all of the lithium, a key component, comes from overseas. In 2020, more than 75% of U.S. lithium battery imports came from China, South Korea, and Japan.[5] The U.S. also imports more than 90% of its raw lithium from Argentina and Chile.[6]

Well, it turns out that the brine of an aquifer under the Salton Lake in California contains enough lithium to economically transform that impoverished region. Perhaps that lithium supply could help the United States surf toward energy independence or at least reduce reliance on China and other countries. Ten geothermal plants and two lithium extraction projects now operate at the Salton Sea.[7]

Those mining concerns have translated their insight about the constraint of U.S. lithium production into action, and they are in the trial, error, and refinement box on the right-hand circle of the Innovation Cycle (Figure 12.1). Validating their ability to safely extract lithium for battery production could help beget success and shift the paradigm, a shift that already has been accelerated by Elon Musk's success with Tesla.

The obsolete paradigm would be gasoline-powered vehicles using the internal combustion engine.

Once most people switch to electric, of course, pipelines will not matter.

This is another example where I disagree with Joel Barker, my mentor on paradigms. Remember, he wrote in the

1980s that paradigm shifters are outsiders. But these mining operators are definitely insiders, people who have a real understanding of mining, lithium, and its importance to the future of cleaner energy.

If you had told me there was a lake with a bunch of lithium under it, my reaction would have been, "So what?"

But knowing that lithium is such a key component of batteries for electric vehicles, phones, computers, and digital cameras, this news makes me go, "Holy cow! That eliminates a constraint and creates a huge opportunity to shift the paradigm from gasoline-powered to electric vehicles."

3. Creating Success from Insightful Leadership

Obviously, all great entrepreneurs have insightful ideas, but the inability to communicate insights, gain allies, and deploy insights often dooms or delays Paradigm Shifts.

Think back to Barker's discussion of the Xerox conundrum (Chapter 4).

That insight wound up on the floor for years because no one thought it was worth anything. Either they viewed electrostatic photography as a new (and inferior) form of photography, or they could not see the value of a plain paper copier. Until the Haloid Corporation realized that xerography would change the way offices work—and it was a major breakthrough and Paradigm Shift—nobody was going to harness the power of that insight.

Having the world's coolest idea is not enough. Insightful Leaders cannot do it alone. They must gather disciples and align a group of people to work together. Only then can they harness the benefits of their ongoing insights, hence the three important steps in creating success from Insightful Leadership: communicating, aligning, and deploying.

- *Communicate:* Widely communicate across your organization your insights, strategies, and innovations to harness the power of your insights.

- *Achieve alignment:* Help the organization grasp the shifts of paradigms and how deploying these developed insights will result in a strong competitive advantage in the marketplace.
- *Deploy insights:* Disrupt the status quo and ride your insights to competitive advantage and major success.

On their way to creating their Paradigm Shifts that beget success, Insightful Leaders must move their organizations through the Innovation Cycle's boxes of "Trial, Error, Refinement" and "Validation" (Figure 12.1). This is the only way to surf the waves to the right market, capture market share, grow, and be successful, setting up your organization to proceed to the next wave and continue through the next time around the Innovation Cycle.

For instance, I had the idea for Tompkins Robotics, covered in Chapter 11. My insider knowledge informed me that eCommerce requires each picking (fulfillment centers that can pick, pack, and ship item by item instead of case by case). I also knew current systems were woefully inadequate for each picking, and you cannot efficiently and cost-effectively deliver eaches to customers by hiring thousands of people to staff a warehouse.

And hiring people to staff a warehouse is quite difficult these days. In the age of the Great Resignation, good luck staffing your warehouse, shipping outfit, or fast-food dining room. It cannot be done. As a result, automation and robotics are a shift that we must embrace, not just because of return on investment but because it's the only way to get orders picked.

I did not build those Tompkins robots myself. I did not know how to make that happen. But I had a solid network of people that I could turn to, communicate that insight with, get them onboard, conduct research (trial, error, refinement), validate that research in the market, and create that Paradigm Shift.

Henry Ford had the insight that automobiles should have been an affordable product for the masses. He did not possess every brilliant idea to make it happen. However, he communicated his insight with enough people who believed, and they helped create a Paradigm Shift, while you and I might have been selling buggies, whips, and horseshoes.

Amazon's Jeff Bezos had no interest in just making an online bookseller. By 2000, the Amazon logo was the now familiar sans serif word "Amazon" with a curved arrow linking the "A" to the "Z," indicating Bezos wanted to revolutionize retail.

He understood exactly where he was going, but he needed to communicate his insights piece by piece, align his team, and deploy his insights to realize Amazon's massive growth potential.

Like everything else in the Insightful Leadership toolbox (or, to continue this book's metaphor, van full of surfboard options), communicating, achieving alignment, and deploying insights works outside of my supply chain/eCommerce specialties.

Take the lockdown Tipping Point that created the work-from-home Paradigm Shift, for example. Working during a lockdown certainly is not my specialty. We had some consultants who worked remotely three or four days a week, but that was because consultants live at their job sites. We had a couple of video conferencing machines, but they weren't used often. We had the old speakerphone in the middle of the desk, 1980s style, as we had never heard of Zoom or Microsoft Teams.

We had a lot to learn. We did. And we have a lot more to learn about the Paradigm Shift of work from home, where your boss wants you in the office but you decide to go work for another boss who will let you telecommute.

Another part of my environmental scanning that helps me

peer around corners involves communicating with a large network developed over decades of work. These people come from a variety of industries—lots of supply chain people, sure, but also those who work in everything from healthcare to artificial intelligence to the roofing industry.

I have talked to hundreds of executives about the necessity of returning to work, and they have policies as varied as all the types and sizes of waves that roll over the oceans.

One very large company I recently spoke to does not have one single policy on returning to work. They first consider how collaborative the job is. Some jobs require high collaboration, while other employees can accomplish at least 95% of their tasks on their own.

Employees with low-collaboration jobs can come to the office one or two days a month. If they want to show up at the office twenty-two days a month, they can, but the suggestion is a day or two. Pick a Monday, Tuesday, Wednesday, or Thursday (not Friday), and then develop a plan. If the dentist or a sick child or a doctor's appointment changes that plan, the employee and the company still have flexibility.

This company's leaders characterize other positions as high-collaboration jobs that require more "facetime," so they require these people to plan to spend more time at the office.

But if their environmental scanning tells them others in the industry do not consider these positions to be high-collaboration, the company knows requiring more office time only guarantees workforce turnover. Face it—IT, data analytics, machine learning, and artificial intelligence specialists can get remote, work-from-home jobs in a heartbeat. So if the company insists that such high-collaboration personnel show up at the office full-time, they will lose those employees.

So, their policy is to consider these factors and do what they think is best. I call this brilliant.

Now, this enterprise must solidly communicate this plan and get buy-in from the workforce, particularly from those required to come into the office who might resent it but not have the work-from-home option others do. Company leaders are right to pay attention to the market because deploying this insight gives their enterprise a competitive advantage in luring talent in a difficult recruiting situation, giving them a better chance to succeed in the new work-from-home paradigm.

Others make decisions on more of a case-by-case basis. I know one organization that allows its technical training director to run operations from Virginia, only visiting its Atlanta headquarters for a week or so every month or two. Others work in the office full-time, and a couple of others show up only once or twice a month because they live in faraway locations.

As for me, I doubt I will ever run an enterprise that employs forty to fifty thousand people, but this is a perfect example of something outside your specialty that's worth paying attention to in order to gain insight that you can use to ride the waves of continual Disruption. It's optionality applied to human resources, and I can certainly use this insight to help build my newest organization, Tompkins Ventures, and assist my clients and partners in adjusting to this Paradigm Shift.

Lastly, let's examine another huge Paradigm Shift in supply chain: the absolutely necessary move to the Digital Supply Networks defined in Chapter 9.

Decades ago, my environmental scanning helped me peer around corners and develop the insight that supply chains would function better if they moved beyond organizational doors and optimized the entire network, from the genesis of every raw material to customer delivery, no matter how many organizations were involved in that process from production to distribution.

I have defined the obsolete paradigm—that everyone in our organization must focus on doing their jobs well and holding our suppliers and customers accountable—and developed a strategy to replace that paradigm: the key to successful supply networks is the level of collaboration, synergy, and teamwork across the network, all working together for the best interest of the entire network.

I widely communicate this strategy with my partners and clients, gaining buy-in and developing the collaborations necessary to align multiple organizations across multiple supply chains into cohesive, linked Digital Supply Networks.

These networks handle high degrees of complexity, eliminate latency with real-time information, autonomously resolve many problems with artificial intelligence and machine learning, use the cloud to optimize the entire chain (not just specific links), and harvest the benefits of internal and external synergies while surfing through a turbulent world of continual Disruptions, Tipping Points, and Paradigm Shifts.

These companies, enterprises, entrepreneurs, and partners involved will disrupt the status quo and change the world forever.

Until, of course, the next change, the next Disruption that moves beyond a Tipping Point into another Paradigm Shift.

What will happen in the future? And are you developing options to give your enterprise multiple surfboards to ride those waves?

Remember how the world reacted when COVID-19 shut down the factory of the world for three months in early 2020 (Chapter 5)? Russia's invasion of Ukraine and its associated supply chain Disruptions are already wreaking havoc. Imagine if China's saber rattling turns into a cross-channel invasion of Taiwan, the epicenter of semiconductor production. What if the 7% inflation rate from 2021 continues for the next few years?[8] What if interest rates for commercial and industrial property double?

How about some other Disruption beyond our current vision? Are you getting your enterprise ready?

Leadership is no longer about having a vision and aligning your enterprise's operations with that vision. Instead, Insightful Leadership for today and the future is about looking around the corner and taking the steps necessary to allow us to get ahead of the competition and create competitive advantage. The greatest opportunity for innovation comes now when history is accelerated. This will be achieved by embracing Insightful Leadership and riding from wave to wave and more.

---

1. "U.S. E-Commerce Share of Annual Retail Sales." *Statista*, 4 Sep. 2021, www.statista.com/statistics/185351/share-of-e-commerce-in-total-value-of-us-retail-wholesale-trade-sales/.

2. Wulfraat, Marc. "Amazon Supply Chain and Fulfillment Center Network." *MWPVL International Inc*, 2022, www.mwpvl.com/html/amazon_com.html.

3. Pickert, Reade. "U.S. Inflation Hits 39-Year High of 7%, Sets Stage for Fed Hike." *Bloomberg News*, 12 Jan. 2022, www.bloomberg.com/news/articles/2022-01-12/inflation-in-u-s-registers-biggest-annual-gain-since-1982.

4. Charan, Ram. "Leading Through Inflation: 5 Priorities For The Company." *Chief Executive Group*, 1 Mar. 2022, chiefexecutive.net/leading-through-inflation-5-priorities-for-the-company/.

5. Suk-yee, Jung. "United States Imports Lithium Batteries Mainly from China." *BusinessKorea*, 9 Mar. 2021, www.businesskorea.co.kr/news/articleView.html?idxno=61880.

6. "U.S. Geological Survey, Mineral Commodity Summaries, January 2022." *U.S. Government Publications*, 2022, pubs.usgs.gov/periodicals/mcs2022/mcs2022-lithium.pdf.

7. Venegas, Guad. "Lithium Under a California Lake Could Help U.S. Gain Energy autonomy." *NBC News*, 18 Jan. 2022, www.nbcnews.com/news/us-news/lithium-california-lake-help-us-gain-energy-autonomy-rcna11656.

8. Pickert, Reade. "U.S. Inflation Hits 39-Year High of 7%, Sets Stage for Fed Hike." *Bloomberg News*, 12 Jan. 2022, www.bloomberg.com/news/articles/2022-01-12/inflation-in-u-s-registers-biggest-annual-gain-since-1982.

EPILOGUE

I have tried hard to get you to think differently about business and entrepreneurial leadership, but the time I invested writing and the time you invested reading is wasted if you do not get off the couch.

One major problem in business today is the prevalence of people like Charlie, for example. Charlie graduated from college thirty-eight years ago and got a job as a warehouse supervisor. His career developed, earning him the titles of warehouse manager, distribution manager, and supply chain manager. Today, he is Chief Supply Chain Officer.

He put four children through college and has a big house, a nice boat, and a place at the beach.

When you go to Charlie with a problem, what's he going to do? The same thing he has done for thirty-eight years. Why?

"Hey," Charlie says. "I got a boat, and everybody has patted me on the back for my success! Why would I ever want to change?"

Unfortunately for the Charlies of the world, the business climate has seen more change in the last two years than in the previous fifty.

You cannot walk around the office waiting, wailing, and wanting to go back to the "normal" of 2019.

You might think you are standing on top of the mountain or relaxing in a canoe on a quiet lake or waiting for the waves to settle down. But you are precariously perched on top of a wave in the middle of the ocean—if your enterprise is not floundering in the surf.

That can be scary, but the solutions are there. Just know that yesterday's solution is not today's solution, today's solution won't be tomorrow's solution, and you'll need to look across the ocean to figure out the day after tomorrow's solution.

You need the insight of Kelly Slater, the youngest (age twenty) and oldest (age forty-nine) to win the Super Bowl of surfing, the Billabong Pro Pipeline in Oahu, Hawaii. He notes that although you deal with many unknowns in the ocean, there is a pattern.

"Get rid of the fear," Slater says. "Understand what the wave is going to do. And become a part of it."[1]

The business world will never be stable again. It is a world of perpetual Disruptions, Tipping Points, and Paradigm Shifts. Grab your surfboard and Go! Go! Go!

---

1. Sneed, Brandon. "Kelly Slater Won the Super Bowl of Surfing at 50. So, What's Next?" *Sports Illustrated*, 28 Jun. 2022, www.si.com/sports-illustrated/2022/06/28/kelly-slater-at-50-daily-cover

ABOUT THE AUTHORS

Jim Tompkins

Jim Tompkins is an international authority on designing and implementing end-to-end supply chains. He has started 15 businesses that have done over $2 billion in worldwide revenue during his 50-year career, has worked with private equity, designed countless industrial facilities and supply chain solutions, and enhanced the profitable growth of numerous companies, giving him an insider's view into what makes great companies even better.

He founded Tompkins Leadership LLC in 2022, focusing primarily on Executive and Board Search, Human Capital and Leadership Development, Organizational Transformation, and Strategy and Innovation. In 2020, he founded Tompkins Ventures LLC, a global hands-on solutions network that helps executive teams turn their five major factors for business success (Leadership, Capital, Technology, Supply Chain, and Facilities) into competitive advantage. He previously built Tompkins International from a backyard startup into an international consulting and implementation firm.

Jim received his Bachelor of Science in Industrial Engineering in 1969, his Master of Science in Industrial Engineering in 1970, and his Ph.D. in 1972, all from Purdue University.

Michael Hughes

Michael Hughes is Vice President of Publications and Communications for Tompkins Ventures. Previously he was Manager, Sales and Marketing and Managing Editor for the Institute of Industrial and Systems Engineers. He also held numerous leadership, editing, and reporting positions at *The Gainesville (Ga.) Times*, *The Burlington (N.C.) Times-News*, *The Sanford Herald*, and *Southeast Magazine*. His writing and editing awards ranged from investigative reporting to Georgia Associated Press Stories of the Year. He started his career as a bartender at The Telegraph Inn and The Green Man in London. His Bachelor's in English is from North Carolina State University.